The Price Is Not Greater Than God's Grace

Oretha Hagin

Unless otherwise indicated, all Scripture quotations in this volume are from the *King James Version* of the Bible.

Fourth Printing 1995

ISBN 0-89276-952-1

In the U.S. write:
Kenneth Hagin Ministries
P.O. Box 50126
Tulsa, OK 74150-0126

In Canada write:
Kenneth Hagin Ministries
P.O. Box 335, Station D,
Etobicoke (Toronto), Ontario
Canada, M9A 4X3

Following God's Plan For Your Life
The Triumphant Church: Dominion Over All the Powers of Darkness
Healing Scriptures
Mountain Moving Faith
Love: The Way to Victory
The Price Is Not Greater Than God's Grace (Mrs. Oretha Hagin)

MINIBOOKS (A partial listing)

* *The New Birth*
* *Why Tongues?*
* *In Him*
* *God's Medicine*
* *You Can Have What You Say*
* *Don't Blame God*
* *Words*
  Plead Your Case
* *How To Keep Your Healing*
  The Bible Way To Receive the Holy Spirit
  I Went to Hell
  How To Walk in Love
  The Precious Blood of Jesus
* *Love Never Fails*
  How God Taught Me About Prosperity

BOOKS BY KENNETH HAGIN JR.

* *Man's Impossibility — God's Possibility*
  Because of Jesus
  How To Make the Dream God Gave You Come True
  The Life of Obedience
  God's Irresistible Word
  Healing: Forever Settled
  Don't Quit! Your Faith Will See You Through
  The Untapped Power in Praise
  Listen to Your Heart
  What Comes After Faith?
  Speak to Your Mountain!
  Come Out of the Valley!
  It's Your Move!
  God's Victory Plan

MINIBOOKS (A partial listing)

* *Faith Worketh by Love*
* *Seven Hindrances to Healing*
* *The Past Tense of God's Word*
  Faith Takes Back What the Devil's Stolen
    How To Be a Success in Life
  Get Acquainted With God
    Unforgiveness
  Ministering to the Brokenhearted

---

*These titles are also available in Spanish. Information about other foreign translations of several of the above titles (i.e., Finnish, French, German, Indonesian, Polish, Russian, etc.) may be obtained by writing to: Kenneth Hagin Ministries, P.O. Box 50126, Tulsa, Oklahoma 74150-0126.

Contents

Preface

Nearly fifty-three years ago when I married Kenneth E. Hagin, I couldn't have imagined God would do all that He has done in our lives and our ministry. If we had known then everything the Lord wanted to do through us, we couldn't have accepted it; the challenge would have been too great. But as we obeyed God and followed Him each step along the way, His plan for our lives began to unfold.

There is a price to pay in order to do the perfect will of God. From the beginning of our lives together, Kenneth and I committed ourselves to do God's will and to pay that price, no matter how great. Now looking back over our lives, I can remember the hard times and the struggles we faced together in the ministry. But I remember those times, not with sorrow, but with great joy. It is so beautiful to say yes to the Lord — to *His* will — and to walk with Him.

No matter how hard life may have seemed at times, Kenneth and I learned that we could not out give God. Payday always came. And looking back, we can say with joy and gratitude that the price was not greater than His grace.

Foreword

By Kenneth E. Hagin

My success in the ministry began with a decision Oretha and I made before we were married to obey God's will for our lives no matter what the price. It all started with our strong commitment to the Lord, but I believe it was also maintained through the years by our strong commitment to each other.

I proposed to Oretha nearly fifty-three years ago. When she said yes to my marriage proposal, she was also saying yes to the call. And for fifty-three years Oretha has been a loyal and supportive wife, and she has faithfully obeyed the call of God on our lives. Oretha's consecration to God and her devotion and dedication to me has been one of the mainstays of my ministry.

Because of Oretha's commitment to me and my ministry, she always trusted my judgment. She always built up my confidence because of her confidence in me and her great confidence in God. Anytime I felt the Lord leading us a certain way in ministry, Oretha encouraged and supported me. It wasn't that I was always right in every decision I made, because I wasn't. But Oretha supported me even when I missed it, and the Lord caused our ministry to grow and prosper.

The way was not always easy for us. We had to endure times of "hardness as soldiers of Jesus Christ" (2 Tim. 2:3). It was during those times that I began to see the wisdom of God in the depth of commitment Oretha and I had made years before to God and to each other. Because Oretha and I always worked together as a team in our marriage and our ministry, we stayed strong in pursuing the call of God upon our lives, even in the hard times. And by God's grace, we have remained steady and determined through the years to *fulfill* the call and to finish the work God has given us to do.

Of course, we know that unless the Lord builds the house, they labor in vain who build it (Ps. 127:1). God is really the only One who can bless a ministry and make it the success it should be. But a wife can make or break her husband in his call in life, and Oretha lovingly supported me in my call. Without her cooperation and support, I could not have done what God gave me to do.

Blessed and happy is the wife who recognizes her place in supporting her husband's call and who faithfully serves God alongside her husband both in the good times and the bad. She is what the Bible calls a virtuous woman, and she will reap a reward with her husband for their obedience to the plan of God for their lives.

To me, Oretha is that virtuous woman. My ministry is her ministry, and my success in life is her success too. The Bible talks about giving honor to whom honor is due, and so it is with love and gratitude that I honor and pay tribute to my lovely wife Oretha. May she be richly rewarded for the continual blessing she has been in my life. And as Proverbs 31:31 says, may "... *her own works praise her in the gates.*"

Foreword

By Kenneth Hagin Jr.

I thank God for my heritage and for the godly example set before me in life by both of my parents. They each positively influenced my life and taught me the value of living for God.

Among other things, Mom taught me the characteristic of *endurance.* She taught me endurance through her own example — through her lifestyle of faithfulness and obedience to God, even in the hard places, and through her devotion and love for my dad.

There were many hardships in the early years of Dad's ministry. But Mom never complained to us about the hardships. And she never magnified the sacrifices we sometimes had to make; she only magnified God's grace. Mom knew how to stay put in the hard places, and she taught my sister, Patsy, and me to do the same.

Faithfulness has always been one of the hallmark characteristics of Mom's life. I remember one day when I was in junior high school, I was complaining to Mom about something that had happened at school. She said to me, "Son, life is not always fair. But if you will live for God and stay true to Him, you will come out on top and be rewarded." I have never forgotten Mom's words or her example, for they have helped see me through many a difficult time in my own life.

Through Mom's life, I learned the importance of serving God wholeheartedly and ministering to the needs of others. But the most important thing I learned from Mom is that *nothing* is more precious or sacred than doing God's will. The God who calls us is indeed faithful!

Foreword

By Mrs. Patsy Harrison

I am a most blessed person because I was privileged to be raised by a virtuous woman. My mother has always lived the Word of God, allowing the fruit of the Spirit to flow through her to others.

My mother showed me how to be a godly woman, wife, and mother. Because of her lifestyle, I knew God and His love were real. I learned prayer and faith from watching her stand in faith over her household. I knew what it meant to be a helpmeet to Buddy because I saw mother be a godly helpmeet to my father.

Truly my mother exemplifies the virtuous woman in Proverbs 31. As verse 28 says, *"Her children arise up, and call her blessed. . . ."* So I bless you, Mother, and thank God for giving me to you. I am what I am today because you showed me the Way — Jesus Christ.

Chapter 1
Faithfulness
Reaps the Reward

Thou therefore endure hardness, as a good soldier of
Jesus Christ.

— 1 Timothy 2:3

From the day Kenneth and I were married, we consecrated our lives to God to do whatever He had for us
in the ministry, no matter what the cost. We began to
understand early on what it meant to "endure hardness
as a good soldier of Jesus Christ."

Kenneth was already in the ministry when we were
married. Many of you have heard him say that before
we were married, he made it clear to me that the Lord
came first in his life. Kenneth said to me, "I love you
more than anyone in the whole world, except the Lord.
I love Him most of all, and I must put Him first. I must
do what He calls me to do. If God says, 'Go to Africa,'
then I must go to Africa. If the Lord says, 'Go to India,'
I will have to go to India."

I loved Kenneth, and I respected him. I also respected
the call of God on his life. I always wanted to be an asset
to my husband's ministry, not a detriment. Although I
knew when I married Kenneth that he was a minister
and had the call of God on his life, I myself knew nothing

1

about the ministry. I said to Kenneth, "I don't have a pulpit ministry, but I am a part of your ministry. I will help you do what God has called you to do." And we've been serving the Lord together in the ministry ever since.

Working in the ministry is wonderful. I wouldn't trade it for anything. But before I was married, I had always said I would never marry a minister. (Don't ever say you *won't* do something for God. You might end up doing that very thing!)

A minister is on call twenty-four hours a day. At one time I didn't want that. But God had something else planned for me, and I said yes to His plan. I'm so glad I did, because nothing could be more rewarding to me than working for the Lord Jesus Christ with my husband.

Everything God did in our lives and ministry had its day of small beginnings. During our first Campmeeting in 1973, Kenneth said by the unction of the Holy Spirit, "We're going to start a training center." Later, Kenneth hadn't even realized what he had said. We had to play the tape back for him so he could hear it for himself! But that's how RHEMA got started.

When Kenneth and I began RHEMA Bible Training Center in 1974, we had no idea it would grow in size like it has and be what it is today. After that Campmeeting in 1973, Kenneth and I went to Indianapolis where we attended one of Norvel Hayes' meetings. After the meeting, a group of us were sitting around a table fellowshipping together. Kenneth was talking to someone else when suddenly Norvel tapped me on the shoulder. The Lord had just shown him a vision of the training center.

"Oretha!" Norvel said, "I see the campus of the training center! It's a big, beautiful campus with lots of students!"

When Norvel said that, I froze. "Oh, no, Norvel," I said, "we don't want that! We just want a small place to teach people who want to go into the ministry — maybe fifty students."

What Norvel said really frightened me at first. I knew what an awesome responsibility it is to be a leader and an example to so many. I didn't want to ever present the wrong example to people or give them wrong advice. Some young Christians get their eyes on ministers so much that if a minister makes a wrong move, they fall away, and some of them never get back on track with the Lord.

I wrestled with the thought of it all for a while. I had to get my will synchronized with God's will. At first, Kenneth didn't want to start a training center either. But the Lord had been dealing with him about it for some time, and the time finally came when Kenneth had to do something about it. I also said, "Okay, Lord. I want to do Your will, not my own." And we obeyed God.

When you're doing what God has told you to do and you're serving Him, it doesn't matter how tough the going gets, God is always faithful. Payday doesn't always come every Saturday night, but if you are faithful to God and His Word, payday always comes. It is just beautiful what God can do for you if you stay faithful to what He has called *you* to do, whether you are called to the full-time ministry or not.

Some of you may be going through hard times in your lives. You may be facing tests and trials, and you may be thinking you cannot take another step in faith or face another day. You may think it's too hard to serve God — that the price is too great to walk in God's will and to fulfill *His* plan and *His* purpose for your life.

But the price is not greater than God's grace. Doing the will of God is worth every test or trial you may face, because when you are trusting God, you will come out of each test or trial victorious. And through every victory, you will become stronger and better equipped to serve God. You will be rewarded if you will make the commitment to stand true to God even in the hard places in life.

God is always faithful, but you have to be faithful to Him too. You can't expect God to be faithful to you while you just do as you please. You've got to be faithful to *obey* God — to obey His will for your life and to obey His Word.

Staying faithful to God takes a lot of prayer. It takes spending time on your knees, seeking the Lord and dedicating yourself to Him. And it takes spending time reading His Word and meditating on it. I think so many times the reason Christians get into trouble and have unnecessary problems in life is that they don't want to spend time seeking the Lord. They want to make their *own* plans, and then they want God to bless *their* plans.

But it doesn't work that way.

Yes, there are times when it may *seem* so much easier to do something other than what God has said to do. But, oh, the rewards of faithfulness! When we say yes to God and we're faithful to do what He says to do, He is so faithful to us, and life works out so much better for us than we could ever have imagined.

I love the scripture, ". . . *I* [have] *not seen the righteous forsaken, nor his seed begging bread*" (Ps. 37:25). Time and time again, I've proven that scripture in my own life. Kenneth and I have been to the place many times where it didn't look like we were going to make it through some of the tests and trials we faced. But God has never forsaken us. He has always been there to see us through and to bless us.

The ministry is not always a bed of roses. Kenneth and I pastored churches for twelve years in the early years of his ministry. And some of those churches were not easy churches to pastor. They were what we called "problem" churches. Then Kenneth began his field ministry, and for the better part of eight years, I stayed home and raised our two young children alone while Kenneth traveled on the road. And it wasn't always easy. There were many lonely hours, many responsibilities, and many decisions to make on my own.

But those days were wonderful times too. Not only did God help me just as He had promised me, but He also blessed our family. God more than made it up to us in the end. Yes, there were pressures. In fact, while Kenneth was gone, there were times I didn't think I could face another day without him. There were times I thought, *I just can't take this any longer.* It was hard for Kenneth, too, although he always said it took more grace for me to stay than it did for him to go. But God's grace was sufficient!

Kenneth and I had a deep desire to serve God. We knew the call of God was on Kenneth's life, and Kenneth had to obey it. But God has been so good to us. Although at times the circumstances may have looked difficult — even impossible — in the natural, we continued to obey God. And God saw us through. Yes, there were times we had it rough from the natural standpoint. But with God, it really wasn't rough. He led us step-by-step. And as we obeyed Him, each step we took in obedience brought us into new areas of blessing and victory.

It may seem as if we made many sacrifices in order to serve God in the ministry. But as the saying goes, it really doesn't *cost* to obey God — it *pays!* It is a privilege to serve the Lord Jesus Christ in the ministry and to do His will. And I thank Him for giving us that privilege.

I never did bemoan the fact that I was a minister's wife or that there were sacrifices to be made because we were serving God in the ministry. I was never sorry we were in the ministry because I knew that's what God had called us to do. We faced some trying times in the ministry, and I can't say I would like to go back in time and do it all over again! But I wouldn't trade those experiences for anything.

Sometimes I remember certain situations and think, *Why didn't I handle that situation differently?* But I always did the best I could with the wisdom God gave me, and I grew in my walk with the Lord. I often look back on the early days and say to the Lord, "Jesus, You were so good to us. I was so ignorant about so many things, and I'm sure I didn't do everything just right. But You were so faithful."

There is nothing more fulfilling in life than to do what God has called you to do. But don't ever think you won't have any tests and trials as you fulfill the plan of God for your life. Jesus said we would have tribulation just because we're in this world. But He also told us to be cheerful because He has overcome the world (John 16:33).

My husband has said many times that we as Christians are not going to just float through life on flowery beds of ease. We are going to have tests and trials. But we serve the Lord Jesus Christ, the One who brings us through every test and trial and gives us the victory!

Yes, the circumstances of life can seem hard at times. But don't be discouraged by the circumstances. If you have chosen to serve God wholeheartedly and to follow His plan for your life, you can rest assured He is directing your course. And when God is directing your course, you can't go wrong in life. Remember, it's in those "hard places" in life where we really come to know God's faithfulness. *God is faithful!* And He will always see us through any test or trial and bless us, if we will trust Him and take Him at His Word.

I thank God for every one of my early experiences because God always brought me through them and taught me through each one to love Him better. And through every test and trial, I learned more and more that God is my Source and that He is faithful.

God is always faithful to us when we are faithful to Him — when we are trusting Him and obeying Him. So be encouraged that as you fulfill your ministry or *whatever* God has called you to do, you're going to reap the rewards of faithfulness.

If you are going through a difficult time and you're thinking, *It's too hard. I'm going to give up because I just can't go on,* realize that nothing is too difficult for God! Nothing is impossible for Him. So put your eyes on Jesus. Hold on to your faith in *Him.* Be faithful to Him in what He has called you to do. He'll be faithful to you, and payday *will come.* And what a rejoicing there will be when payday comes. If you won't quit, you'll be able to say, "Thank God, I didn't forsake Him, because He hasn't forsaken me."

God will never forsake us. We may forsake Him, but He doesn't forsake us. God loves you regardless of what mistakes you've made in the past. And He loves you regardless of what you *haven't* done for Him that perhaps you *should* have done. If you'll return to Him, He'll receive you, and He will always be faithful to you.

Knowing how much God loves you and cares for you, you can determine in your heart, "I *will* make it." And then from that point, do whatever God tells you to do. But you can't be halfhearted about your commitment to do God's will. If you are halfhearted, in time you may forget about your commitment to the Lord and begin doing something else instead of serving Him.

Remember, we can't make our own plans and expect God to bless our plans. Instead, we are to let God give us *His* plan, and we are to follow *His* plan for our lives. As I said, so many times we want to make our own plans because we have made up our minds we want to do things our own way. But let's get it right! Let's follow *God's* plan for our lives. God's plans are right, and it is so wonderful and rewarding to follow Jesus. He is so sweet and lovely, and He is so loving and kind.

Over the years many people have asked me, "What is the key to your success?" There are many keys to success in the ministry and in life. But I always tell people that first, you have to be willing *and* obedient to do what God has called *you* to do.

Second, I tell people that in order to remain willing and obedient to God through the good times and the bad, you've got to be *faithful*. You've got to be faithful to serve God. And you've got to be faithful to obey God and His Word.

I encourage you to be faithful to obey God and to follow His leading step-by-step. If Kenneth and I hadn't been faithful in the early days of our ministry — even in the small things — we would never have accomplished what we have accomplished today. And being faithful in the small things doesn't just apply to people who are in the ministry. It applies to all of us. If you are faithful to do what God says to do, God will be faithful

to bring you into all that He has planned for you. So
stay faithful and remain steadfast in the vision God has
given you.

Galatians 6:9 says, *"And let us not be weary in well
doing: for in due season we shall reap, if we faint not."*
Don't faint by the wayside in your commitment to the
Lord. Stay in the fight of faith because you are the vic-
tor in Christ. You won't lose as long as you are walking
with Him. Jesus will always see you through. You may
think you're going to go under because of the storms of
life, but you won't. Just trust Jesus, and He will bring
you safely through every storm.

In order to succeed in life — whether or not you're
called to the ministry — you can't quit doing what God
has put in your heart to do. You can't obey God for a little while and then quit when the circumstances don't
look too good or when your faith is being tested and
tried. You've got to be faithful to carry out God's plan
for your life.

I think the reason many people fail in life is that
they get impatient. But you can't get impatient in the
things of God. The plan of God for your entire life won't
unfold overnight.

Many times, God will tell you something about the
future, and you want it right then — or yesterday! But
God has to get you ready for what He's called you to do.
You might not be ready right now to handle what God
has for you. But God will get you ready and steer you in
the right direction. And if you will follow the gentle
nudge you have from the Holy Spirit, then step-by-step

He will lead you until He gets you to the place spiritually where He knows you are ready.

So be patient as you fulfill God's plan for your life step-by-step. Even when things don't happen the *way* you think they should or *when* you think they should, faithfulness is what will bring you through to victory in God. The devil may try to stand in your way to see what you are made of, so to speak. But that's when you will have to stand fast and show that you mean business with God. God never fails. And no matter how difficult the test or trial, faithfulness *always* reaps the reward.

Chapter 2
From Test to Testimony:
Grace for Every Day

I was born in Blue Ridge, Texas, and grew up in White Mound which was a little farming community near Sherman, Texas. I grew up on a farm where my daddy raised cotton and corn. There was only one country store in White Mound, so we always went to Sherman on Saturdays to do our shopping, run errands, and spend time with family and friends.

As a young child, I attended the local Baptist church in the neighboring town of Tom Bean, Texas. I attended church with my mother, and I remember I was eight years old when Mama went forward to the altar and got saved. Four years later, I went to a Methodist tent meeting with both of my parents. I remember I was standing between my mother and dad during the altar call that night when the Lord spoke to me. He told me to go forward and give my heart to Him, and I did.

Later I began attending a Methodist church with one of my girlfriends and her family. I was faithful in my church attendance, and as a result I believe I helped influence my father to give his heart to the Lord too. Soon after my father was saved, we began attending a Pentecostal church because Daddy seemed to like it better.

When I began attending the Pentecostal church, I

was uneasy at first because I wasn't used to all the shouting, tarrying at the altar, and loud singing the Pentecostals did in their meetings. But after a while I got used it, and I had no reservations about attending. I remember watching some of the older ladies in the church. Sometimes they would get so excited about the things of God that they would shout until the hairpins flew out of their hair!

Those were some of my first encounters with the Pentecostal church. Little did I know what lay ahead for me and that this would only be the beginning of my Pentecostal experience. At that time I could not have dreamed I would one day be serving the Lord in the ministry as a Pentecostal preacher's wife!

In the summer of 1938, I was away visiting my aunt when the new pastor, Rev. Kenneth E. Hagin, came to our home church in Tom Bean, Texas. He was tall, slim, blonde, and handsome — and all the single girls in the church were after him!

I remember the first time I ever laid eyes on Kenneth. I was standing outside the church with some friends, and we peeked through the window to get a look at our new pastor before going inside.

I looked through the window at Kenneth, and there he stood behind the pulpit, immaculate. He was wearing a light grey suit and a white shirt that was ironed to perfection. Every hair on his head was in place. Immediately, I whispered to my girlfriend, Mary Jo, "He's mine if I never get him!"

Soon after Kenneth and I met, our courtship began.

On Saturdays Kenneth would ride into Sherman with the family he lived with, and I would ride into town with my family. Kenneth and I had our first dates in the very back corner table of Skillern's Drugstore there in Sherman where we would fellowship over pimiento cheese sandwiches and malted milk. That's how we got to know each other. The courtship lasted from June to November. We were married November 25, 1938.

At that time, I hadn't received the Holy Spirit, although secretly I had wanted to. During our courtship, Kenneth would always say to me, "I'd marry you tonight if you had the baptism of the Holy Ghost." When Kenneth would say that to me, I would just look at him and smile. He married me anyway, because I didn't receive the Holy Spirit until *after* we were married!

My father had met Kenneth before I had, and Daddy loved this young preacher from the beginning. Daddy believed in Kenneth and always encouraged him to pursue his call in the ministry. When Kenneth and I were married, Daddy invited us to make our home with him and my mother for a while.

On the fourth night after we were married, Kenneth and I were praying together with my parents in the living room, and the Lord spoke to Kenneth. The Lord told Kenneth to lay his hand on my forehead and I would receive the Holy Spirit.

The Lord had never said anything like that to Kenneth before, and at first Kenneth was kind of hesitant about doing that. But after the third time the Lord spoke to him, Kenneth lightly touched my forehead with his left hand, and I instantly received the Holy Spirit and began to speak in tongues. Kenneth said I spoke in tongues for about an hour and a half that night and sang three songs in other tongues.

It was on that same night that I sensed the Lord telling me that one day Kenneth would be gone. I thought it meant Kenneth would die, so I pushed the thought aside. It was ten years later when Kenneth went into the full-time traveling ministry that I finally realized what the Lord was saying to me that night.

Kenneth and I began our married life in the ministry. In 1939 we moved from Tom Bean, Texas, where we lived with my parents, to Farmersville, Texas, where we began pastoring a church. The supernatural move of God was still new to me, and the people at that Pentecostal church in Farmersville seemed especially on fire for the Lord! They would get out in the aisles and start dancing and shouting in the Spirit, almost at the drop of a hat.

You've probably heard Kenneth tell the story of the young girl who walked back and forth across the altar bench at the close of one of his services, speaking in tongues and exhorting sinners to get saved. That girl kept her eyes closed during the entire altar call, and every time she reached the end of the bench, it looked like she was going to step off. But she always stopped just in time and turned and walked to the other end of the bench, her eyes closed the entire time!

That incident happened in the church at Farmersville. Every sinner in the place got saved that night.

Afterwards, the girl — her eyes still shut — stepped off one end of the altar bench and began dancing in the Spirit in mid-air!

It was exciting to see what God could and would do when His Word was preached. Kenneth always honored God and His Word, and it was just beautiful what God did in some of our services. Even though the supernatural move of God was still new to me, I had already come a long way — from being a young Methodist girl who knew nothing about the ministry to becoming the wife of a Pentecostal preacher. But each step of the way in the ministry, I learned I still had further to go in my walk with God. It was precious to be able to walk with God the way we did and follow His plan for our lives.

Growing up, I had always been my Daddy's "baby." Our family wasn't rich by any means. Those were the Depression Days, and jobs and money were scarce. But my father made a good living as a farmer, and if I wanted a new dress, Daddy always made sure I got it.

Kenneth told me before we were married, "Sugar, I won't be able to dress you right now like your father did because I'm just starting out in the ministry." I told him that would be all right, and together we set out to do the will of God.

When we got married Kenneth had one dime, and you've probably heard him tell how we went to town the next day and bought a candy bar for each of us. So, you see, we started on the bottom. We couldn't go anywhere else but up! We determined to obey God and follow His plan for our lives, and we've been going up ever since!

About four years after Kenneth and I were married, we attended a ministers' convention in Houston. We had a car, but we didn't have enough money to buy gasoline to attend the convention. Some of the other local pastors in our community were supposed to ride with us to the convention and help with the expenses, but at the last minute they decided not to go. We used what little money we had to buy gas, and we ended up at the convention with no money for a hotel room.

At the convention Kenneth decided to apply for assistance from a ministers' fund so we could rent a room. As he went to apply, he met one of his old friends. This friend had also been a pastor but was no longer in the ministry because he had taken a job at one of the local shipyards in order to make more money.

Kenneth's friend invited us to stay with him and his wife during the convention, and we accepted the invitation. During our stay at this couple's house, this man and his wife kept telling us how well they were doing financially, and the wife showed me all her new clothes, including a new coat with a fox fur collar.

I didn't even have a coat, not even an old one. And I only owned one dress that wasn't frayed and that was decent enough to wear in public. I'd had to borrow clothes from my sister-in-law just so I could attend the convention.

Up until that time I had never complained to Kenneth because the way was hard and the price seemed so great to obey God's will and serve God in the ministry. But that night when this woman showed me all her new clothes, I went into the bedroom where we were staying, and for the first time, I cried because I didn't have any clothes and didn't even have a coat.

Kenneth sat down on the bed beside me to comfort me. He put his arms around me and said to me so sweetly, "Sweetheart, we are in the work the Lord has called us to do. If we continue to be faithful to His calling, He will bless us with more in the end than anything these people have ever had."

I'm so glad I made the decision to support my husband in the ministry. As we have obeyed God, not only have our lives been blessed, but our ministry has expanded to reach around the world with the message of faith in God's Word. And God has given us many precious souls for the Kingdom of God!

Kenneth was always faithful to preach God's Word. Even when it looked like the Word wasn't working in our own lives, Kenneth kept at it; he kept preaching the Word. It didn't happen overnight, but step-by-step God brought us forth into His perfect will for our lives and has blessed us in more ways than we could have ever imagined.

So, you see, we didn't start at the top in the ministry. Many people look at us today and think we've always had it easy. But we didn't. There were many lean years. But God had called Kenneth. We knew God had something for us to do, and we were faithful to stay with the vision God had given us.

Kenneth's friend who had quit the ministry to make more money later died while working in a welding shop.

He was in his fifties. He had tried to get back into the ministry, but he could never seem to make a go of it. God could have blessed that man so much if he had stayed with what God had called him to do. That's why it's so important not to get your eyes on money, but to keep your eyes on the Lord. If you will stay faithful to God even in the hard places, He will bring you through to victory. God is your Source!

People are wrong when they depend only on man and think they've got to have money before they can do anything for the Lord. If you're doing what God told you to do, and if you're trusting Him, He will supply your every need.

As Kenneth has said many times, payday doesn't always come every Saturday night. And things won't always happen for you when you think they should. But if you're faithful to God — if you are obeying what God has told you to do — payday will always come. It came for us, and it will come for you, too, if you will obey the Lord and be faithful to His call on your life.

In the early days of Kenneth's ministry before I met him, people used to call him "the walking Bible." Kenneth never went to Bible school. He educated himself in the Word through diligent study. He wanted to attend Bible school, but the money he needed just wasn't there when he started out in the ministry. At that time Kenneth didn't have the revelation of believing God for finances like he had for believing God for healing.

Kenneth bought books written by godly men of faith to help him in his studies. Many of the books he bought were used in Bible colleges and seminaries. Many times after I had put the children to bed and had gone to sleep myself, Kenneth would stay up studying until very late. Sometimes he would study all night long. We didn't have a study in our home — just a desk in the corner of our living room. Later when Kenneth began his field ministry, he would take a suitcase full of books with him on the road, and he would study at night in his hotel room.

Kenneth was faithful to study God's Word, and Kenneth's faithfulness to God's Word has paid off in the ministry. Kenneth was faithful to *obey* the Lord too. For example, I remember even in the early years when there wasn't much money, sometimes the Lord would speak to Kenneth to give a personal offering to certain ministers. One time the amount was about half of what we had received for the entire week, so it was a sacrifice to give it. But Kenneth was faithful, and he obeyed God and gave to that minister.

Then one time a minister came to our church at Christmastime. All of his family members attended that service, including his in-laws. He was timid, and he wouldn't preach because he didn't want to preach in front of his family. The Lord told Kenneth to give that minister ten dollars. That was a lot of money during the Depression Days.

Kenneth argued at first, "Lord, I can't give that man ten dollars. I haven't even bought my wife or children anything for Christmas yet." But he obeyed God and gave the man the money, and we had a wonderful

Christmas that year.

Later in January, that man's mother-in-law testified in our church. She said, "When my son-in-law was here for Christmas, he only had enough money to pay utilities and rent. He didn't have any money for Christmas, not even for Christmas dinner. But the Lord blessed him with some money, and it was enough to buy Christmas dinner, plus a gift for each of his four children."

When this woman testified, Kenneth didn't jump up and say, "I did that! I did that!" If he had, he would have lost his reward. But because of Kenneth's obedience, God blessed us and we had a happy Christmas, and that family had a happy Christmas too.

Kenneth's obedience paid off in the long run too. Years later we ministered to a woman on her deathbed who had been given up to die, and she was miraculously raised up and healed. The Lord told Kenneth that if he hadn't been faithful to obey Him in giving to those two ministers even in the hard times, He couldn't have used Kenneth in this woman's healing.

It certainly pays to obey God, even in the small things. If you obey God in the small things, the rewards will be great. There is nothing more rewarding in life than to fulfill God's perfect will and to be a blessing to others. So no matter how little money you have, if God asks you to give, then give! And if God asks you to give of your time, obey Him. You will be rewarded for your obedience — maybe not the next day or the next week — but you *will* be rewarded.

We witnessed some beautiful moves of God's Spirit

in the churches Kenneth and I pastored. Kenneth and I had a wonderful marriage, and our home was like Heaven on earth. Since we started out in the ministry with nothing, everything we had we received by faith, and we were so happy.

The early years were some of the most wonderful and exciting years we spent in the ministry, but they were some of the hardest years too. The victories did not come without the battles and the tests. As I said before, the ministry is not always a bed of roses. Sometimes we have to endure hardness for a while in order to do the perfect will of God.

For example, I remember one parsonage Kenneth and I lived in. It was a little shotgun house — only three or four rooms lined up in a row from the front to the back of the house. The parsonage wasn't painted, and the walls pulled away from the floor in places so you could actually see outside through the cracks! We had to stuff paper in the cracks to keep out the cold wind.

There was no running water inside the parsonage or any plumbing of *any* kind! We had a wood-burning stove in one room of the house, and in the wintertime that room was the only warm place in the house! We had only one blanket to keep us warm until my mother brought us some quilts she had made.

There were times when we didn't have any wood for the stove, and the stove was our only source of heat in the house. One cold winter night when we didn't have any firewood, we heard a knock at the back door at about midnight. Kenneth got up to answer the door, and there stood a sinner man with an arm load of fire-wood. God had spoken to him and told him to bring us some wood because we didn't have any! As Kenneth says, thank God a sinner can listen to God sometimes even when Christians don't listen to Him!

We had to endure some hardships in the ministry. But I never complained to Kenneth because I knew God had His hand on Kenneth. God had healed Kenneth of a deformed heart and an incurable blood disease and had raised him off a deathbed. I knew God had called Kenneth into the ministry. And I had promised to help Kenneth fulfill that call.

Some of the parsonages we lived in and the places we stayed as we traveled over the years were not always the best. The conditions were not always good. But we didn't complain. We took those opportunities to use our faith, and we would just thank God for a better place to stay next time. And God always provided for us and blessed us, and He saw us through the hard times.

Kenneth and I had pastored about ten years when the Lord began dealing with Kenneth about going into the field ministry. Kenneth kept putting it off until the Lord finally asked him, "What are you going to do about what I've told you to do?" Kenneth told the Lord he would obey Him, but Kenneth also told the Lord that He would have to prepare me first.

I had never told my husband what the Lord showed me ten years before on the night I received the Holy Spirit. The Lord had already shown me that there would come a time when Kenneth would be gone and I would be left alone. I didn't understand it then, so I just put the thought aside, and over the years I had refused to even think about it.

But then Kenneth began praying and seeking the Lord about a change in his ministry, and I began praying about it too. As I prayed, the Lord showed me what He meant when He'd told me ten years earlier that Kenneth would be gone. So when Kenneth asked me if the Lord had been talking to me, I told him what the Lord had said years before — that Kenneth would have to be gone. It was so wonderful how God always prepared both of us each step of the way for what lay ahead in the ministry!

Those first years Kenneth was gone ministering in the field were very difficult for both of us. As I said, we had a wonderful marriage, and our home was like Heaven on earth. Pat was in the second grade and Ken Jr. was in the third grade when Kenneth went out into the field ministry. It was difficult raising the children alone because with Kenneth gone, I had to try to be both mother and father to them for about eight years.

I was young, and I didn't know how to do that. I could not possibly have raised our children by myself, but the Lord was right there to help me through it all, especially in the difficult times. He was so gracious and faithful to me, and I grew to love Him so much.

Traveling in the field was hard on Kenneth too. Kenneth had come from a broken home, and he never really knew his father. His father had left his mother with four small children to raise when Kenneth was only six years old. So having a home and a family always meant a great deal to Kenneth.

I remember when Ken Jr. was born, the first time Kenneth saw him, he took him ever so gently in his arms and dedicated him to the Lord. Then Kenneth asked me how soon it would be before the baby could go places with him! It was the same way with Patsy. Kenneth loved his family very much, and he was a wonderful father to the children.

Kenneth and I had never been apart before, and when Kenneth went into the field ministry, it was difficult not seeing each other. There were times when I would have given just about anything to see him. Just to talk to him and say hello would have been so wonderful. We didn't make many phone calls in those days because we didn't have much money. But we wrote each other a love letter every day.

Although I received a letter from Kenneth every day, it was still very lonely without him. Sometimes when I was alone, I would cry and complain to God, but never to Kenneth.

I had accepted the fact that Kenneth would have to be gone from me and the children, and I thought I had totally consecrated myself to the will of God. But sometimes we wouldn't get to see Kenneth for four or five weeks at a time. One morning after the children had gone to school and I had begun to clean the house, I cried to God in desperation. I complained, "Lord, I just can't take this anymore."

Later that morning as I was washing the dishes, I

heard a Voice say, "I could take him where he would never come back." (This didn't mean *God* would kill him, but our disobedience would leave the door open for the enemy to come in and attack us.) That startled me, and I went throughout the house, searching for who said that. Then I decided it was just my imagination.

I had never said a word to Kenneth about this or about how I had complained. Being gone so much of the time was hard on him too. Kenneth knew God had called him to go on the road ministering, and he had obeyed that call. But the time came when the price of leaving his family seemed too great, and Kenneth decided he could not continue to pay that price.

Kenneth had been out on the field for about six months, and I had been at home with the children when we decided Kenneth should come off the road. Kenneth cancelled all of his meetings and decided to try out as pastor for a church in east Texas.

On Sunday morning, July 10, 1949, we visited that church. Kenneth attended the men's Sunday school class and I attended the ladies' class. During Sunday school, I suddenly became so uneasy, I could hardly sit still. I sensed in my spirit that something was wrong.

I wanted to leave the class to go see about Kenneth, but I didn't know where the men's classroom was located. I had already gathered my purse and my Bible to leave when the pastor came into our classroom and motioned for me. As I reached the door, he whispered, "Come to the parsonage immediately. Your husband has had a heart attack and he's asking for you."

My heart raced and my mind was in a panic as I made my way to the parsonage. All I could think was, *Dear God, it's my fault for grumbling and complaining about Kenneth being gone so much. I know I helped bring this on.*

I rushed to Kenneth, and when I got there he was close to death. In fact, when some of the men had sent for me, they couldn't detect a pulse. I saw Kenneth lying there on the bed, his face as white as a sheet, and there was cold, clammy sweat on his brow. I put my hand on his heart, but I couldn't feel a heartbeat. I began to cry, and I fell down beside the bed and began to silently repent to God.

I told the Lord, "Forgive me for grumbling and complaining because Kenneth has been gone so much. I know it was You who spoke to me in an audible voice that morning while I was washing dishes. I cried and complained to You, and You said, 'I could take him where he would never come back.'

"Forgive me, Lord," I continued. "Just spare his life. Just let us keep him. I'll never grumble and complain again. I don't care where he goes or how long he stays away doing what You've called him to do."

I found out later that Kenneth had already repented for disobeying, but he still thought he was going to die. When we had both repented and consecrated ourselves anew to the Lord, Kenneth was instantly healed. He got up off that bed and danced all across that parsonage floor!

So with renewed consecration, Kenneth and I agreed

to do God's will — from our hearts this time, not from our heads. Then the Lord said to me so sweetly, "I'll give you grace for every day." And He has!

You see, *we* were the ones who decided that Kenneth would cancel his meetings and come off the road. But that wasn't *God*'s plan; it was *our* plan. And, really, from the beginning we both knew in our hearts that taking a church was not what God wanted us to do.

I thought I had already said yes to God's will from my heart, but I realized I really hadn't. I had only said yes from my head. But God was so merciful. After we repented, we went back to what God had told Kenneth to do concerning the field ministry. And we have remained faithful to the call and to the plan of God ever since.

As I said before, it doesn't really *cost* to obey God; it *pays*. But just because God tells you to do something for Him doesn't mean it's going to be easy every step of the way to obey what He's told you to do. When God tells you to do something, you may have to make some sacrifices in order to obey it. But in the end, it will always pay. Kenneth and I have proven that in our lives time and time again.

I spent practically eight years all by myself while Kenneth was out ministering. The kids and I hardly ever got to see him during that time, and when we did, it wasn't for very long at a time. Kenneth used to preach in meetings right up until Christmas. Sometimes he would make it home on Christmas Eve. But he always tried to be with us during Christmas for about a week before he'd have to leave again. Traveling full time in the ministry was a big sacrifice to make, but God told Kenneth to do it, and God's grace for us was sufficient each day.

You see, Kenneth wasn't traveling out on the road just to be doing it. He would rather have been at home with us. But God said, "Go," and Kenneth obeyed. He had to do what God had called him to do. It was a life-or-death proposition with him.

When you've got a message burning in your heart and you know what God has called you to do, you can't sit still in disobedience. You have to get out and preach the gospel and share what God has put in your heart. And if you are not faithful to obey God, God won't be able to fulfill His promises to you. He wants to, but He won't be able to because if you're not faithful to His Word, what does He have to make good in your life?

Yes, God is merciful, and if you have missed it, God will be gracious to you if you will return to Him with all of your heart. But God can't bless disobedience. We've got to be faithful to God's Word and to His will for our individual lives. It's as my husband often says, "If you will stand by God's Word, His Word will stand by you. But if you don't stand by God's Word, God doesn't have anything to make good in your life." How true that is.

Even though there were times in our ministry when we had no money and very little food or clothes, we just kept on being faithful to what God had called us to do. And God always came through for us. When you're doing what God has told you to do, it doesn't matter how rough the going gets, God is always faithful. He's faithful to me, and He will be faithful to you, too, if you will obey Him and trust Him.

God always made a way for us in the hard times and gave us grace for every day. I remember one time Kenneth and I were three months behind on our rent. I knew we were in God's perfect will, but we didn't have enough money to pay the rent or to buy enough food or clothes for the children. I didn't understand that then, but we didn't have the revelation back then that we have now about exercising faith for finances. We just trusted God where we were at in our faith walk, and God was so gracious to us.

It was no coincidence that our landlord was a pastor who believed in Kenneth's ministry, and he wanted to help us! He would let Kenneth pay the rent late, when the money came in. You see, if you will remain faithful to your call, the faith life will work for you no matter where you're at in your walk with the Lord.

God gave me grace for every day during the hard times in the ministry. I always had peace, and I never doubted that Kenneth and I were in God's perfect will. It was hard being apart from Kenneth while he was on the road. But finally in 1955, we sold all of our furniture and bought a travel trailer, and for the first time, we ventured out in the field as a family.

I was thrilled to be in those meetings on the road with my husband. It was such a joy and a blessing to hear God's Word taught and the prophecies the Lord brought forth through Kenneth. Just the fact that God would use us was overwhelming to me. God didn't use us because we were somebody special; we were just His vessels. But it was exciting to know that we were allowed to be a part of what God was doing in the earth.

We traveled as a family for fifteen months. During this time in the field, Ken Jr. and Pat were taking correspondence courses, and Kenneth taught them their lessons in addition to preaching and teaching in his meetings. I would have lunch ready when he returned from his morning meetings. After lunch I would clear the table, and Kenneth would sit down with the children for about three hours, and they would have school. Then we would rest for forty-five minutes or an hour before getting ready for the evening service. That was almost always our daily routine.

Pat fared pretty well living in a travel trailer, but it was hard on Ken Jr. because he was very athletic and active. Traveling on the road with the children during the school year was hard on Kenneth, too, because he took a lot of time with the children, teaching them their lessons in addition to preaching and teaching in his services.

In 1956 the children went to a private Christian school in Oregon, and I traveled full time with Kenneth in the field. Ken Jr. and Pat were both in high school by then. They attended the boarding school in Oregon for one year before we returned to Texas where later they both graduated from high school.

God was always faithful to show us His plan for our lives one step at a time, and we prospered as we fol-

lowed Him and obeyed His plan. In 1963 while praying
and seeking the Lord in a little church in Houston,
Kenneth received more of the plan. Kenneth began to
be overwhelmed by the immensity of the work that was
before him. He knew the message of faith in God's Word
had to be brought forth to the whole world. Kenneth
cried out to the Lord and said he couldn't do it by himself — it was too big a task.

The Lord told Kenneth, "You don't catch any fish out
of your own bathtub." Then the Lord showed Kenneth
that he was just going in circles traveling from church
to church to minister. The Lord said to Kenneth, "Start
a radio ministry. Go on the radio and teach, don't
preach. And get all of your lessons into print." And that
is how Kenneth Hagin Ministries, as it is known today,
got started.

In 1966 we moved from Garland, Texas, to North
Utica Street in Tulsa, Oklahoma. We lived in an apart-
ment located above our ministry offices. Our children
were grown, and I traveled in the ministry full time
with my husband. We would be away for as many as
three months at a time, and when we got home again,
we would be very tired.

Even though we had an unlisted telephone number,
people would see our car parked in front of the offices
and would come to visit Kenneth at all hours of the day.
We had very little privacy or home life at all.

One morning in January while I was making the
bed, I was overcome by all the pressures of not having
any privacy, and I fell on my knees by the bed and

prayed. "Lord, please give me a house," I prayed. "Please give us a home before the year is up."

The following May while Kenneth and I were away on a Holy Land tour with the Full Gospel Business Men's Fellowship, the Lord sent an Episcopalian woman whom we had never met to our offices. She told our son-in-law, Buddy Harrison, who managed our offices, that the Lord had instructed her to buy us a home!

This woman not only bought us a beautiful home, but she contributed generously to help us redecorate it. And in August of the same year I had asked the Lord for a house, we moved into the home He had given us! That experience just proved to me again that if you're faithful to do what the Lord calls you to do, He makes life so exciting and rewarding.

When you walk with God, sometimes He may ask you to do things you don't want to do or that seem difficult or impossible. For example, RHEMA Bible Training Center became a reality in September 1974, but in the natural, it was a project that both Kenneth and I hesitated to start. Kenneth did not want to have a school at first, but the Lord dealt with him about it, and Kenneth made the decision to obey. I wanted to obey God, too, but I knew what a great responsibility it would be.

The Lord had been dealing with Kenneth for some time to start the training center. Training men and women for the ministry was to be a large part of Kenneth's vision of taking the message of faith to the world.

But at the time Kenneth obeyed the Lord and began the training center, we were not at all aware of the magnitude of what the Lord was going to do through the school.

In 1975, 58 students graduated from RHEMA's charter class. This year in 1991, 827 students graduated from the training center. Since RHEMA started, more than 12,000 students have graduated from RHEMA to enter the harvest fields for the Lord.

When RHEMA first started, we never dreamed RHEMA would grow to the size it is today. But God had His own plan. And as I had already learned from being in the ministry for many years, God's grace was sufficient! With God, nothing is too difficult. So with God's grace and His guidance, we began RHEMA Bible Training Center.

RHEMA actually began in classrooms located in Sheridan Christian Center in Tulsa. We spent a considerable amount of time looking for property to purchase for the training center. Finally, one of our board members showed us the property where RHEMA is now located. We knew in our spirits that it was the right property for the campus. After we made the purchase, we learned of fifty more acres that were available adjacent to our property, so we purchased that too.

We made the first purchase in July 1976, and by God's grace, we finished the first classrooms in September, in time for the fall term. Since then, RHEMA has grown so much it's almost unbelievable. The RHEMA campus sits on more than ninety acres of property, and it's a beautiful sight to me every time I see it. And God did it all. It wasn't Kenneth and me because we are only God's vessels. But starting RHEMA was God's plan for us. When you obey the Lord and fulfill *His* plans and purposes, your ministry — whatever it is — will grow beyond all that you could ask or think.

Today our ministry continues to grow. Kenneth doesn't talk about retiring. In the past he has talked about slowing down, but we haven't really done that yet either! We both plan to stay active until we go to be with the Lord or until the Lord comes again.

Looking back over the years, I can honestly say that God has been faithful to lead us one step at a time. And as we were faithful to obey Him, God would show us more of His plan. Because we obeyed God, we can now look back and see all that He has been able to accomplish in our lives. He truly has given us grace for every day just as He promised. And He has turned every test into a testimony of His faithfulness and love.

Chapter 3
Setting a Godly Example
In the Home

When the Lord told Kenneth to begin ministering in the field, we decided that I would stay home and provide a proper home atmosphere for our children. We didn't want our children to travel in the ministry when they were young. We wanted them to be in school so they could get an education and learn how to get along with other children.

We also wanted our children to be in school so they would know how to live in the world. Christians may not be *of* the world, but we certainly live *in* the world (John 17:12-16). We knew our children would have to go out into the world someday and learn how to face life and still hold on to their faith. Regardless of how much parents try to shelter their children, their children will still have to face life one day.

It's sad when a child is completely sheltered from the world, because one day when that child is grown and is ushered into a world that's so big, he won't know what to do, and he could go in every direction but the *right* direction in life. It's sad to see children grow up and not be prepared to meet the challenges they will have to face.

So I stayed home for about eight years while Kenneth traveled in the ministry, and I made a home for our children. Of course, we traveled together as a family during the summer months when the children weren't in school.

Raising children is a calling in itself. There are many challenges involved in raising children, especially if you are a single parent, or a mother like I was whose husband traveled in the ministry. I had to be both mother and father to our children while my husband was gone. I kept the children in school and provided them with a good home environment. But I also made sure our children had a good church family. We always attended church faithfully, even when Kenneth was gone.

It's so important to be faithful in your church attendance. Kenneth and I have always been sticklers for the local church because whether you are in the ministry or not, every Christian needs a church home. God designed the church as a place where we can be fed spiritually and taught the Word of God. That doesn't mean you can't be fed spiritually in your own devotions and Bible reading at home. But without attending church, you just can't grow as a Christian like you should.

During the time Kenneth was away ministering, I took Ken Jr. and Pat to church practically every time the church doors opened. Our children never put up a fuss, because they had been trained all of their lives that attending church was not an option! On Sundays my children never asked me, "Mama, are we going to church today?" because it was always a rule in our house that we would go to church.

Ken Jr. and Pat always looked forward to going to

church. They *wanted* to attend church, and they wanted to associate with the right kind of friends who loved the Lord like they did. I think one of the reasons my children were that way was that I kept them in church as young children, and that's where they made most of their friends growing up.

I was always very interested in the friends my children chose. When Ken Jr. and Pat were growing up, I knew the friends they were associating with. And I usually knew where my children were and what they were doing because they would almost always invite their friends over to our house for fellowship! There were many, many weekends and afternoons after school that our house was full of young people! But I liked it that way.

I always told Ken Jr. and Pat, "Bring your friends here for fellowship. Anytime you want to have them over, the house is always open." That's what a home is for — to be lived in and enjoyed. After all, who was I making a home for if not for my family?

I always let Ken Jr. and Pat have fun when they brought their friends to our house. I wasn't afraid the house was going to get dirty, and I didn't constantly nag them about it. Yes, sometimes the house got a little messed up. But I always taught my children how to clean up their messes, so that was never a problem!

It's not wrong to be particular about the way your house looks. In fact, you *should* want your house to look nice, and you should do everything you can to make sure it is clean and kept up. If you don't clean your house up and keep it looking nice, that will carry over into other areas of your life; it shows that your life is not in order. Life is not *all* spiritual; practical things are important too.

So it's not wrong to keep your house clean and looking nice. But it is wrong to be so fussy and particular that your children can never have their friends over or have any fun in their own home. There are more important things than having a perfect house all the time. A house can always be cleaned up. But it is so important to provide a happy home for your family. If your children grow up in a good home atmosphere, they will always have pleasant memories of home even as adults.

So I knew where my children were and who they were with because we always opened our home to our children's friends. And, of course, when our children weren't home, I always knew where to find them. (Ken Jr. loved sports and was always very athletic. So if he wasn't at home, I knew I could always find him wherever there was any kind of a ball game going on!)

No, I didn't know everything my children did, and my children weren't perfect. But I did my best to see that they were keeping the right company because if children begin socializing with the wrong crowd, they will start picking up bad habits that can be very harmful to them.

Even though I knew who my children's friends were, that didn't mean I kept my children under my thumb and didn't allow them to think for themselves or have any freedom. It is good for children to make some decisions for themselves because it will help them cope with life better when they are older.

I believe it's better to teach children the difference between right and wrong than it is just to teach them a lot of do's and don'ts. If you teach your children the difference between right and wrong, they will be able to make right decisions when they are out on their own. But if you just teach your children do's and don'ts or a set of rules they don't understand, they could grow up and rebel against you and God.

Our children were always taught to respect the things of God. They were also taught to respect the call of God on their father's life. Our children understood what God had called their father to do because we shared it with them, and we made them feel they were a part of fulfilling that call.

Ken Jr. and Pat never complained or resented the fact that their father was in the ministry and couldn't be at home with them as much as he would have liked. Naturally, it wasn't easy for them, but they were always really sweet about it. That doesn't mean our children didn't miss their father, because they missed him very much. But they understood what God had called him to do, and that helped a lot. We tried to provide a normal home life for Ken Jr. and Pat, and they were happy children.

Kenneth tells the story of the time he took Ken Jr. on the road with him over spring break holidays. One night Ken Jr. cried and asked his dad why he couldn't be at home like other fathers. Kenneth gently explained why, and then they got on their knees and prayed together. That settled it for Ken Jr. He understood and never questioned again why his dad couldn't always be at home with him.

Having a daddy who traveled in the ministry was harder on Ken Jr. than it was on Pat. I think it's harder for little boys to be apart from their fathers because boys need that father image growing up. But Ken Jr. was so wonderful about the fact that his father was in the traveling ministry.

Ken Jr. didn't gripe and complain, but sometimes I could look in his little face and know that he wished his daddy were there. I'm sure there were many things Ken Jr. wanted to talk to his daddy about that he couldn't talk about with me. It made my heart hurt to see that. But because I knew *God* had told Kenneth to go into field ministry, it made it easier to be faithful. The Lord saw us through those difficult times, and He has more than made it up to us over the years.

Many times there are sacrifices that have to be made in the ministry. But if you complain because of the sacrifices, it will leave the wrong impression on little children.

For example, there were many times when Kenneth was away that we had just a few dollars to last us for a week or longer, until Kenneth could preach his next meeting. But I never complained to Kenneth, and I never told the children we didn't have any money. For all they knew I always had a pocketful of money!

There were constant demands for money for the children because they needed clothes, school supplies, and extra money for school and church activities. I would always say to God, "Lord, You're going to have to stretch this money somehow because I'm not going to deprive my children." And God would always make a way; He would always come through because He's so faithful. And my children weren't deprived.

I never did bemoan the fact that we were in the ministry and that we had to make sacrifices. Yes, there were times when we had no money and very little food and the children didn't have many clothes to wear. But we always made it through the hard times. The hard times were *never* greater than God's grace for us.

So although we had to sacrifice in the ministry, we taught our children that it is wonderful to serve God. We didn't want them to have a bad image of the ministry. I have seen many pastors' wives say, "My poor kids. They have to sacrifice because we're in the ministry, and they can't do this, and they can't do that."

I never told our children we couldn't afford to buy them the things they needed. Kenneth and I always told our children that God would meet our needs. So if I told them we couldn't afford the things we needed, they would think, *Well, God didn't come through for us.* I didn't want them to think that way because God will always come through for us when we look to Him and trust Him. God is *always* faithful.

Our children learned about the faithfulness of God as they grew up. Not only did they respect the things of

God, they were very respectful and attentive to Kenneth and me and precious to us in every way. Kenneth taught them the Word when they were young, and while he was away, the children and I never failed to read the Bible and pray each day before they went to school.

Patsy was a very quiet and sweet child. Ken Jr. was like his dad — very lively, but always a gentleman. Even in his teenage years, Ken Jr. was very attentive to me. For instance, he always made sure I wasn't alone on holidays and special occasions.

The Lord blessed our family in so many ways because we were obedient to His will. Both of our children were saved and filled with the Holy Spirit at an early age, and they both loved the Lord with all of their hearts.

I didn't really prompt either one of them in their decisions for the Lord. I let God do that. All I did was encourage them to serve God and be faithful to their home church. Kenneth and I felt it was our duty to teach our children about faithfulness in the small things when they were young, because we knew it would help them be faithful in other things as they grew up.

If you train your children and put the Word into them when they are young, they may make some mistakes as they are growing up, but they won't be swept away by the world. Even if they do make mistakes and begin to stray from the Lord when they are older, they will come back because of the Word you've instilled in them.

Yes, children have to be allowed to be children, and

teenagers have to be allowed to be teenagers. And they won't always do things perfectly. They have to grow up, just like everyone does. But if you teach your children properly and show God's love to them when they're young, they won't ever stray very far from the Lord, even when they are older.

It's important to train your children in the things of God, but it's also important to pray for your children even as they are older. If you do your part at home and if you pray for your children, then even when they are tempted to do wrong, they will have that little "tug" of the Holy Spirit on the inside of them to lead them in the right way.

I remember when Ken Jr. was in Taipei, Taiwan, serving in the U. S. Army during the Vietnam War. He once wrote me a letter, thanking me for the right example that both Kenneth and I had set before him when he was a child. He thanked me for keeping him in church all those years when his father was ministering on the road — times when it would have been so easy not to attend church regularly.

In his letter Ken Jr. said that he had been tempted to do some things that were wrong while he was overseas, but that he just couldn't do them because of the example that had been set before him when he was younger. What could be more rewarding for a mother than to know her children are walking with the Lord as adults because of what they learned in the home as small children!

Of course, discipline plays a big part in raising children too. And discipline begins in the home, not in the church or school. I was the disciplinarian in our house, mainly because I was with the children more than Kenneth was. As I said, my children were not perfect, but they were never too hard to discipline. They were very obedient, and they never rebelled against Kenneth and me.

I think one reason some children are disobedient and rebellious is they don't see the right example set in the home. Many times they don't see the God-kind of love demonstrated by their parents. For example, if a husband and wife don't walk in love toward each other, it will be evident to their children. It will show. A husband and wife who don't show love to each other are setting the wrong example for their children.

If you as a parent don't show any love to your spouse, how can you expect your children to show love to others? But if a husband and wife are loving and kind toward each other, their children will grow up to be loving and kind too.

Whether you want to believe it or not, your children will do what *you* do. They will imitate you because what they see in you is all they know. After all, who else is going to train your children but *you*, their parents? So set the right example and walk in love toward your spouse and your children.

It's so important for parents to live the Christian life before their children, especially if they're in the ministry. In his early days of ministry, Kenneth saw many ministers who didn't do that. They set the wrong example in front of their children, and it hurt those children spiritually.

One way a parent can set the wrong example before their children is by gossiping and being critical of others. But you should never talk badly about others, especially in front of your children. You might think your children are too young to understand what you're saying, but as they get older, they are going to understand, and they will remember how you talked about other people.

One time when Ken Jr. was about twelve years old, Kenneth took him on the road with him to a meeting because Ken Jr. had a school holiday. They were staying in the parsonage at the church where Kenneth was ministering. One day as they were all sitting at the dinner table, the pastor of that church began talking badly about some of his church members and deacons. Kenneth said he kept watching Ken Jr. to see how he would react. Finally, Kenneth said to this pastor, "I would rather you cuss in front of my son than to criticize other people in front of him."

What this pastor said about his church members and deacons may have been true, but talking in a negative way about other people leaves the wrong impression on little minds. If children hear their parents gossiping and criticizing others, then they could grow up thinking that kind of behavior is all right. But it's not.

We should pray for others, not talk about them. We need each other's prayers. Praying for others is a part of walking in love and setting the right example. But if you don't walk in love, and you are always gossiping and being critical, your children will do the same things because you are their example.

As I said, some parents — even ministers — don't set the right example before their children. And they don't show their children the God-kind of love. Some parents are either too harsh toward their children or they don't pay any attention to them at all. But children who aren't shown any love will grow up not knowing how to give or receive love properly.

Kenneth and I always determined we would show our children a lot of love and not lose them for the sake of the ministry. We have seen so many ministers' children who grew up and rebelled against God and fell away from God because as young children they were neglected by their parents. So Kenneth and I decided we wouldn't let that happen in our home.

Before we were married, Kenneth and I discussed how we would raise our children. One of the things he said to me was, "Why should we go out and get other people's children saved and let our own children go to hell?" We decided then that our children would never be neglected.

Kenneth's home life was destroyed when he was a young child. His father left his mother with four young children to raise. Kenneth's mother eventually had a nervous breakdown and lost her eyesight and was no longer able to care for them. So Kenneth was practically raised as an orphan, with some of the children living in one place and some of them living in another place. Kenneth always looked forward to the time when he would grow up and have a family of his own.

Kenneth started to preach when he was seventeen years old. In those days, a preacher who was invited to a church to speak usually stayed in the pastor's home. One thing Kenneth noticed when he stayed in ministers' homes is that many ministers and their wives would be so busy with the work of the ministry that they often neglected to minister to their own children.

Some of these ministers would come home after a long day and have no time to spend with their children. Many times these ministers would be tired after a hard day's work, and they would be irritable and hard to get along with. They would take their frustrations out on their children, and the children would suffer for it.

That's one reason I always made my family my first priority. When our children were very young, it took most of my time just to care for them.

I attended the ladies' meetings, but I made sure my children didn't suffer because I was too heavily involved in church work. It was my place to make sure my children were properly cared for *first*, before I concerned myself with the work of the ministry. I was still a part of my husband's ministry because I supported him and prayed for him, and I kept things running smoothly at home. But Kenneth and I determined we would put first things first and not neglect our children.

One thing I did do with my husband was to accompany him during church visitation. Kenneth never did a lot of visitation as a pastor because he always taught the people to get into the Word themselves and believe God for themselves. They grew in the things of God, and they didn't need to be prayed for or counseled all the time. If our church members needed us, we were there for them because that was our responsibility and we loved them. But we didn't baby them by continually visiting them.

Also, Kenneth would never visit or counsel with a woman if the woman was alone, because the devil could use that to start tales and rumors. It just isn't a good idea for any man who is a minister to visit or counsel with a woman alone. Kenneth always expected me to help him in this area, so I went with him to do visitation.

Keeping house and raising children is a full-time job, so when I accompanied Kenneth on church visitation, he would always help me with the housework. Kenneth would do most of the housework while I bathed and dressed the babies. We always took the children with us on church visitations, or we took them to my mother's house because we didn't have a baby-sitter at that time (we didn't even know what a baby-sitter was back then!). And since Kenneth helped me with the housework, when we left to do visitation in the mornings, the parsonage was always in tip-top shape.

We always tried to raise our children according to the Word of God, and from the time our children were very young, we began teaching them about God.

I remember before our children ever started school, Kenneth would read children's Bible storybooks to them. Ken Jr. could answer every question in those books. He would just rattle off the answers. Pat was different in nature than Ken Jr. She would sit and listen to Kenneth read, and she knew the answers too. But Pat was shy and didn't like to answer the questions out loud like Ken Jr. did.

We trained our children in spiritual things, but we trained them in natural things too. Children need to be trained in every way so they can be prepared to get out on their own when they grow up. For example, I taught both of our children how to do housework when they were young; I would put them to work helping me wash and dry the dishes. Children should be taught how to handle responsibility because that builds confidence in them.

I think ministers' children have more responsibilities growing up than other children because ministers' children are always expected to set a good example. That is a big responsibility. It may not always be easy, but if a minister's children will be faithful to the Lord themselves and be faithful to their parents' call, they will be rewarded too.

I would always tell my children, "Don't ever do anything that would make a bad mark on your daddy's ministry. Keep your lives right with God and walk uprightly before your friends and set the right example." Yes, I knew Ken Jr. and Pat were normal children and that they were sometimes going to get into mischief (Ken Jr. used to say he thought I had eyes in the back of my head!). My children weren't angels; they weren't perfect by any means. But they respected the things of God, and they tried to set the right example before others.

When Ken Jr. and Pat went away to a private school for a year, they attended classes with many other preachers' kids. As Kenneth often relates, Ken Jr. would come home and tell his father that the biggest problems the teachers had in school were with the preachers' kids. Ken Jr. would say to his father, "The kids' parents never had any confidence in them, and the kids just lived up to the parents' expectations of them."

In Bible college Ken Jr. noticed the same thing. Ken Jr. started driving a car when he was sixteen years old. Some of his college friends would ask him, "You mean your daddy let you drive the car when you were sixteen?" "Of course," Ken Jr. would tell them. "When I was sixteen, I drove my mom and my sister all the way from Texas to Oregon."

Many of Ken Jr.'s friends said, "My dad never let me drive the car. My dad would scream and holler if I even *asked* to drive the car." That's not good because doing that shows children that their parents don't trust them, and that hurts their self-confidence.

Always assure your children when they are very young that they will amount to something. If you haven't always done that, you can begin *now* to build confidence into your children. No matter how bad your children seem to behave now, don't ever tell them they won't ever amount to anything. That tears down their self-confidence. You have to *build* confidence into your children. And you do that by training them, by giving them responsibilities, and by trusting them to do what you've given them to do.

As I said, many times in the ministry, parents spend so much time working for the Lord that they forget to teach and train their own children. But children need to be trained in natural ways and in spiritual things too. They need to be taught how to live the Christian life, and they need to learn how to believe God's Word for themselves. Children don't learn those things automatically. They have to be taught. And teaching your children builds confidence into them because it shows them you care about them enough to spend time with them.

Parents should not only teach their children, but they should set a godly example before them. Parents should show God's love to their children, but they should show natural love, too, because children need affection. It's a sad thing for children to be raised in a home where no love and affection is shown.

Kenneth and I have always shown love to our children, and Kenneth and I have always been deeply in love with each other too. The day we were married, the first thing Kenneth said to me after we left the church was, "We'll always be sweethearts." And we have been sweethearts ever since.

It was that way with us because we wanted it to be that way, and we worked at it. Even when we had to be separated while Kenneth was out on the road, we remained sweethearts. During those years Kenneth was gone so much, we wrote each other a love letter every day. In our case, "absence did make the heart grow fonder" because our love became sweeter every day that passed! Kenneth has always been a thoughtful and loving husband to me. He always remembers my birthdays and special days, and every day, he is gentle, kind, loving, and helpful in every way.

Kenneth is a wonderful father too. Growing up, our children adored their father, and it is no wonder, for Kenneth was always a gracious and sweet father to them. He not only taught them about the Word, but he lived the Christian life before them.

As I said, children will usually become what their parents are. Most children want to be like their parents — daughters want to be like their mothers, and sons want to be like their fathers. That was true with our children too. Ken Jr. especially wanted to be just like his father. He even wanted to eat the same foods his father ate. At restaurants when he was young, Ken Jr. would ask Kenneth, "Dad, what are you ordering?" and he usually ordered whatever his father ordered. Ken Jr. wanted to be like his dad and follow his example.

It's not true in every case, but most of the time when children stray from the Lord and get into trouble, it's because a right example wasn't set in their home. I think another thing parents can do to set the right example for their children is to keep their children in church and Sunday school and attend church regularly themselves.

You may not think your children are learning anything in children's church, but children are very smart.

They learn more than you think they do. A young child may be writing or coloring or drawing during church, but you'd be surprised how that child can tell you exactly what the teacher said in that service!

Raising children is a big responsibility, but with the Lord to help you, you can be successful. As parents, there may be sacrifices you will have to make for your children, but whatever you do, don't sacrifice the well-being of your children. Any sacrifice you might make for your children is not too great a price to pay to be sure your children have the best life possible.

I have found that if you let Jesus guide your life, and you walk closely with Him, you will set the right example for your children, and things will go well for you and for your children. Even if you make a mistake and the circumstances don't always look good, those circumstances will change if you will keep your attitude right and trust God to work things out for you.

But if you are always disgruntled, and you're always gossiping and criticizing others, or if you're griping and complaining about your husband and your children because nothing ever suits you, then you're in bad shape spiritually. If that describes you, you need to return to Jesus and just let Him love you back to the place you were with Him before.

I have found that if your spiritual life isn't what it should be, then your physical life and your emotional life will sometimes suffer too. Your physical energy will be low when your spiritual life is low. But life is just so much sweeter when you're walking closely with the

Lord, loving Him and doing what He wants you to do. And life will be sweeter for your family too!

Parents have a big part to play in how their children turn out in life. The Bible says, *"Train up a child in the way he should go: and when he is old, he will not depart from it"* (Prov. 22:6). I believe that's true. The Bible also says to bring your children up *". . . in the nurture and admonition of the Lord"* (Eph. 6:4). Neglecting your children and setting the wrong example before them is certainly not bringing them up in the nurture and admonition of the Lord.

Kenneth and I never worried about our children straying from the Lord as they were growing up. I'm not bragging on us; I'm bragging on the *Lord*. After all, without Him we can do nothing. He helped us raise our children, and He can help you raise your children too.

As I said before, our children weren't perfect. We were a typical family with typical children. We just mixed all of their ups-and-downs growing up with a lot of love. And with the wisdom of God to direct us, we got them raised. Actually, Kenneth and I always say that we grew up with our children!

We have always been a very close family and a very loving family. In spite of the times we were apart while Kenneth was traveling in the field, our family was always able to remain close through the years. And we are still close today. In the early days, there were four of us until our niece, Ruth, came to live with us when she was sixteen years old. Ruth was with us for so many years, she became a part of the family.

God has more than made it up to us for the times our family was apart. Both of our children and their families are working for the Lord in the ministry. And we have a beautiful family — five grandchildren and three great-grandchildren.

The Bible says, *"Delight thyself also in the Lord; and he shall give thee the desires of thine heart"* (Ps. 37:4). God certainly has given Kenneth and me the desires of our hearts! After all, what more could you desire than to have your entire family working for God in the ministry, getting souls saved and teaching people God's Word?

Today Ken Jr. and Pat are still very attentive to Kenneth and me, even though they have families of their own now. And they are still precious to us in every way! I thank God for both of my children. They've always put God first in their lives, and I thank God for that.

Of course, there were many trying times raising a family in the ministry. But we stayed faithful to God and to His plan, and it paid off. The rewards of the ministry have been great.

Our ministry has certainly grown from its days of small beginnings when we pastored our first church in 1939. And not only has God blessed the ministry we have today, He has blessed our personal lives too. Kenneth and I weren't perfect parents, but by God's grace, we tried to set a godly example before our children. And as we obeyed God's will and His plan for our lives, He was faithful to bless us and keep us strong and close as a family all these years.

Chapter 4
A Note to Wives:
How You Can Support
Your Husband's Call

In like manner you married women, be submissive to your own husbands — subordinate yourselves as being secondary to and dependent on them, and adapt yourselves to them. So that even if any do not obey the Word [of God], they may be won over not by discussion but by the [godly] lives of their wives,

When they observe the pure and modest way in which you conduct yourselves, together with your reverence [for your husband. That is, you are to feel for him all that reverence includes] — to respect, defer to, revere him; [revere means] to honor, esteem (appreciate, prize), and [in the human sense] adore him; [and adore means] to admire, praise, be devoted to, deeply love and enjoy [your husband].

— 1 Peter 3:1,2 (*Amplified*)

Since the beginning of our marriage, I have always felt that my mission in life was to stand by my husband's side and help him fulfill the plan of God for his life. In our marriage, I've always wanted to minister to the minister! And I still feel that way. When Kenneth and I were married, we became one; I have a part in my husband's ministry. I don't have a *pulpit* ministry, but I tell people all the time that I've been in the full-time ministry for almost fifty-three years!

When I married Kenneth, I didn't know anything about the ministry, although I had faithfully attended church and Sunday school as a little Methodist girl. Kenneth had already been in the ministry about four years when we married, so he had a little bit of experience. The Lord had raised Kenneth off a deathbed just four years before, and Kenneth had committed his life to obey God and to preach the gospel. Kenneth made it plain to me before we were married that he would have to obey the Lord, no matter what the Lord called him to do or where He called him to go.

I agreed to obey the Lord too. That didn't mean I was going to do what God had called my husband to do because I didn't have a pulpit ministry. I wasn't called to preach. But obeying the Lord *did* mean I would *help* my husband do whatever God called him to do. And it meant I would go with Kenneth wherever God called him to go.

It's been said that a wife can either make or break her husband in the ministry or in whatever God has called him to do. A wife can either believe in her husband and help him, or she can criticize him and hinder him in his call. In Genesis 2:18 the Lord says, ". . . *It is not good that the man should be alone; I will make him an HELP meet for him.*" A wife is a "helpmate" to her husband. She is called to stand beside her husband and *help* him, not *hinder* him. And she should support her husband's call first, not her own interests or desires.

There are many ways a wife can support her husband's call and help him fulfill the plan of God for his life. But through the years I found that the most important thing I could do to help my husband fulfill his call was to pray for him.

When Kenneth and I first started out in the ministry together, we pastored several churches over a period of ten years. It seemed as though the Lord always led us to pastor churches that had problems no one else had been able to solve. I think God led us to these problem churches because Kenneth is a man who walks in the peace of God and who trusts God in every situation and circumstance. And Kenneth is a man of prayer. He never makes any big decision in his life or ministry without seeking God first and getting God's wisdom.

With God's help Kenneth was always able to deal with any crisis that would arise in those churches we pastored. We watched God bring those problem churches out of difficulty, and they were good, stable churches when we left them.

Pastoring was not always an *easy* task, but it was always a *rewarding* task. It was wonderful to see people in our church grow in the things of God and in their walk with the Lord. And as a pastor's wife, it was fulfilling for me to know that the people were growing spiritually because of the Word of God my husband fed them and taught them. Kenneth couldn't have pastored those churches like he did without God's help. But we prayed and we sought God, and God was always faithful to bless and help us.

The Bible says, ". . . *The effectual fervent prayer of a righteous man availeth much*" (James 5:16). Anyone can pray halfheartedly about something. But to be effectual in prayer, you need to be earnest and consistent. So, wives, pray for your husband and his ministry or call. Hold the situations of his life up before the Lord, and ask God to strengthen him so he can do God's will.

In Exodus chapter 17 the Bible talks about Aaron and Hur supporting Moses by holding his hands up while the Israelites were in battle. As long as Moses held his hands up, God caused Israel to prevail against the enemy. But when Moses grew weak and couldn't hold his hands up anymore, Israel began to be defeated (Exod. 17:11,12).

When you pray for your husband, you are "holding his hands up" spiritually, like Aaron and Hur held up Moses' hands. And when you pray, God will strengthen your husband so he can continue to do the will of God in his life and be victorious. There is power in prayer!

If you're not already praying for your husband, I encourage you to support your husband through prayer. If you are faithful to take your place and fulfill your call as a helpmate to your husband, God will reward you because He's faithful. But if you don't support your husband in the ministry or in the call God has given him, you won't have any reward.

Yes, there is a price to pay to stand with your husband and support the call of God on his life. It won't always be easy, and there may be times you will feel like giving up. Those are the times you need to draw your strength from God. The Lord is so loving, and His love will never fail you. He will give you grace for every day. But if you're always nagging your husband and pulling him in the opposite direction from the direction in which he should be going, he won't be able to accomplish very much for the Lord.

In 1949, the Lord led Kenneth to leave the church we were pastoring and begin traveling in the field ministry. For eight years Kenneth was gone most of the time. It wasn't always easy for me because I was left alone to raise two children. But I didn't complain to Kenneth about it. I didn't make things harder on him, because he didn't want to be apart from us either. From the day we were married, I had chosen to obey what God had told Kenneth to do. I had made a commitment, and I stayed with it because I knew God had called Kenneth and that God's hand was on Kenneth's life. I didn't want to hinder my husband in any way. I wanted to be in agreement with him and with the plan of God for his life.

Philippians 1:27 tells us to ". . . *stand fast in one spirit, with one mind striving TOGETHER for the faith of the gospel.*" I think some people have misinterpreted this scripture because I have seen husbands and wives who were striving *against* each other! This shouldn't be, because how can two walk together unless they be in agreement (Amos 3:3)?

You may not fully agree with everything your husband believes God has called him to do, but you can still pray for him and stand with him. God will show your husband what to do. You don't have to strive against your husband because God can't bless that. God can't bless strife, but He *can* bless agreement, harmony, and unity.

If you are having problems staying in agreement with your husband about what God has called him to do, ask God to help you. If you mean business with God and you are sincere, God will help you obey His will, and He will bring to pass His plans and purposes for your lives. God will use you in greater ways than you could ever have dreamed, if you will only obey Him.

Even if your husband does make a mistake in following the Lord's leading, don't ever condemn him. If he misses it, he'll probably be battling enough condemnation from the enemy. So don't ever say, "I told you so." Just continue to pray for him and stand by his side. God can turn the situation around and make it right again because He is bigger than our mistakes!

I've always been supportive of whatever God told my husband to do. I just always purposed to stay in agreement with Kenneth and to pray for him. And I determined to stand by him in accomplishing whatever task the Lord set before us.

There can't be two leaders in your marriage or in your ministry. Remember, a wife is a *help*mate, called to stand beside her husband and *help* him. And she should put his ministry and call first before her own.

For example, a pastor's wife is called to help her husband fulfill his duties as a pastor. She does not have authority over her husband, and she shouldn't have the last word when a decision needs to be made in the church. Over the years in the ministry, I have seen some pastors' wives try to usurp authority over their husband in the church. I have actually seen them try to run the church service from the front row! Some of these pastors' wives would actually tell their husbands when it was time to quit preaching in the service!

This kind of behavior is very distracting, and it is also very humiliating for the pastor. He has the message from God for the people, and he knows what God wants him to do in the service. He doesn't need to be hindered or distracted by someone on the front row telling him what to do!

The Holy Ghost directs a service through the person behind the pulpit — through the *speaker* — not through someone sitting on the front row. And the Holy Ghost knows when it's time to quit! If you are a pastor's wife, you may think your husband is preaching too long or that he's missing it in some way in his preaching. But don't criticize him. There may be a time to offer *constructive* criticism to your husband, but during the service is not the right time!

If you are trying to direct a service one way, and your husband has something else on his heart for that meeting, there won't be any order in that service, only confusion. And God is not the author of confusion (1 Cor. 14:33). So be sensitive to the Holy Ghost, and be sensitive to your husband.

If you are pulling against your husband in a service, it

will hinder the move of the Holy Ghost in that service. Besides, that kind of behavior is *very* unbecoming. The people in your congregation will lose respect for you if they see you usurping authority over your husband. Yes, it's important that you attend services with your husband and help him in whatever way you can. But as a wife, you are called to *support* your husband, not dominate him.

Kenneth and I began our married life in the ministry. We were married in November 1938 and began pastoring the church in Farmersville in 1939. As I said, when I married Kenneth, I didn't know anything about the ministry or about being a minister's wife. So at first, I did a lot of listening and very little talking! When I got an opportunity, I observed other women who were in the ministry. I learned a lot that way — both how to act and how *not* to act!

For example, I saw many pastors' wives who just talked all the time. They would repeat gossip to just about everyone in their church, and they kept rumors going constantly. God is not happy with that kind of behavior because He doesn't like strife and confusion. God likes unity and harmony, and He wants us to walk in His divine love. But when someone is gossiping and spreading rumors, there can't be unity and harmony. Gossip will only bring strife and confusion, and sooner or later it will cause division.

I learned as a pastor's wife to be very careful who I befriended in the church because it is so important to your husband's position as the pastor that you use caution when talking to members of your congregation. For example, something you say could be misunderstood by someone, and if he or she repeats what you've said, it could cause strife and confusion, and the effects could be disastrous for your church.

So if you are a pastor's wife, be careful what you say to the members of your congregation. As a pastor's wife, it is usually not a good idea to make close friendships with members of your church. It is usually wise to find another pastor's wife in your community to be your friend. And if you ask God for friends, He will give you good friends who are quiet and discreet and who know how to pray — people who won't gossip and betray your confidence.

Mom Goodwin was someone like that for me. The Lord sent Mom Goodwin my way to teach me and to be an example to me. She was a pastor's wife, and she became my example in the ministry because she was truly a woman of God.

I observed the way Mom Goodwin conducted herself in public, in the church, and in her home. I always noticed that she never usurped authority over her husband, Rev. J. R. Goodwin, although God used her in the ministry too. She was a gracious woman and a fine example of a minister's wife, and I admired her very much.

Mom Goodwin walked by her husband's side, and she helped him in the ministry. She worked alongside her husband in the ministry, but she always respected him as the leader and as the head of their home.

Mom Goodwin greatly respected Brother Goodwin's call and his position as the pastor of their church. For example, when church workers would ask her a question about something they wanted to do in the church, she would always say, "Let's go ask Dad; he's the pastor." Mom Goodwin always stayed in agreement with her husband's call. She shared her husband's vision for his ministry. That's so important because the Bible says a house divided against itself cannot stand (Matt. 12:25).

I learned a lot about the ministry by watching others and by being teachable. It's important to always stay teachable. If you ever get to the place where you think you can't learn something new, then even God won't be able to help you because you're not teachable.

First Peter 3:4 says, *"But let it be the hidden man of the heart, in that which is not corruptible, even the ornament of a meek and quiet spirit, which is in the sight of God of great price."* It is very important to God *and* to your husband that you develop a meek and quiet spirit, because if you have a quiet spirit, God can get through to you and teach you the things you need to know. But you can't learn if you won't listen.

One of the greatest secrets I've learned in the ministry is the importance of loving people. If you want to see people's lives touched and changed by the Lord, you must love them. The Bible says love never fails (1 Cor. 13:8). Kenneth and I have always endeavored to walk in love, even when others wronged us. And it made a difference in our ministry because God can bless a person who walks in love.

Over the years, many women have said to me, "I know I'm supposed to help my husband in the ministry, but I'm called to the fivefold ministry too." If you and your husband are both called to the ministry, remember, your husband is still the head of your home. You can work side by side with your husband in the ministry and still honor him as the head of the home in your marriage. Yes, you can have your own ministry if God has called you. But if you try to push ahead of your husband in the ministry and compete with him and usurp authority over him, that will eventually carry over into your home life, and you will have problems.

As my husband has said, anything with two heads is a freak. So if you are called to a ministry of your own, be patient. Let your husband take the lead. Don't try to push out ahead of him in the ministry. If you will put first things first and honor your husband as the head of your home, and if you will put your husband's ministry first, God will take care of your ministry.

"Yes," someone said to me, "but what if I'm called to the ministry and my husband is not?" If you are called to the ministry and your husband isn't, make sure you include him somehow in your ministry. Don't ever make him feel inferior because he's not called to the full-time ministry. In other words, don't act like you are better than he is because of the call of God on your life. And *don't* neglect your husband for the sake of the ministry, because he is your first priority. Remember, your husband is still the head of your home.

If you are a wife, your first ministry is to minister to

your husband. That includes ministering to his physical needs, but it's more than that. As a helpmate you are called to help your husband — to encourage him and to "hold his hands up" — and to support him in what God has called him to do.

You are also called to be a godly example of a Christian wife. The world is always watching us as Christians to see how we behave ourselves. They want to know if we believe what we say we believe about living holy and right before God. The world especially watches people who are in the ministry. I have said many times that being in the ministry is like living in a fish bowl because your life is constantly on display. That's a big responsibility.

We are responsible for the way we present ourselves and conduct ourselves before others. And as ministers, we must walk worthy of the call of God on our lives. So don't deceive people in your Christian walk. In other words, don't say you believe the Bible, but then act like you don't really believe it. Walk in the light and *walk in love!* We are to walk like Christ and talk like Christ and let His love flow out to those we meet. The Bible says, *"By this shall all men know that ye are my disciples, if ye have love one to another"* (John 13:35).

You might ask, "What does all this have to do with supporting my husband's call?" It has a lot to do with supporting his call, because your life and the example you set is a reflection of his life, too, since you and your husband are one. Your behavior and your lifestyle will affect, good or bad, the way others see your husband.

That's why I never talk badly to others about my husband. I always speak words of praise about him, and I lift him up. I'm sure some people think Kenneth has angels' wings because of the way I talk about him! But I never belittle my husband or speak unkind words about him to others. Yes, Kenneth is human just like anyone else. And, yes, he makes mistakes. But my husband is the most important person on earth to me. And I think he's the most *wonderful* person on earth too!

I trust my husband. I believe in him, and I adore him. He is a wonderful husband, father, and minister. And he knows how to hear from God. Kenneth seeks God first and puts God first in our lives, and Kenneth never makes an important decision in life until he knows he has heard from God.

Kenneth makes this his practice. I've seen him live his life before God this way ever since we've been married. And to me the most important quality a woman could desire in a man is that he really knows God and has a close walk with Him. Also, it's important that he lives a consecrated life before God and is sensitive to God's leading.

I believe in my husband. I love and respect him, and I want to please him in every way. I want to take care of my spiritual life because that pleases God *and* my husband. But I want to look attractive for my husband too.

Some Christian women have thought it wasn't important to keep themselves attractive for their husbands because of First Peter 3:3 and 4. In the *Amplified* translation it says, "Let not yours be the [merely] external adorning with [elaborate] interweaving and knotting of the hair, the wearing of jewelry, or changes of clothes. But let it be the inward adorning and beauty of the hidden person of the heart. . . ."

We wives shouldn't pay more attention to our physical appearance than we do to our inward man because God says a meek and quiet spirit is what is truly precious in His sight (1 Peter 3:4). But First Peter 3:3 *doesn't* mean that wives are to neglect their physical appearance altogether either!

Some people think this scripture means wives are not to be concerned with keeping their hair fixed, wearing makeup, or keeping themselves groomed and attractive for their husbands. But that's not true. Yes, you are supposed to develop your inward man and have a meek and quiet spirit. As I said, having a quiet spirit is important both to God and to your husband. But your physical appearance is also important, and you should want to please your husband in this area too.

Keeping yourself attractive is another way you can minister to your husband and show your support for him, because looking your best shows him you care about him and want to please him. For example, your husband will not think you want to please him if he comes home from work in the evening and sees you looking the way you did when you woke up that morning. In fact, he may want to turn around and go back to work!

Most women don't look their best when they first wake up in the morning. I usually wake up in the mornings before Kenneth does, and the first thing I do is have private devotions, shower, dress, and put on my makeup. Kenneth usually prepares breakfast for us both, and I always go to the table looking nice for him. It just makes my day when my husband says to me, "You sure look beautiful this morning." I don't know about you, but I look more attractive with makeup than I do without it!

You might say, "But I have small children, and I don't have time to always look my best." You may not have time to always look your best, but you *can* take some time to make yourself look nice for your husband. When your husband looks at you in the morning and kisses you, you will feel better knowing you have done something to make yourself more attractive to him. A husband wants his wife to look nice, and a wife should want her husband to look nice too.

A wife should pay attention to her physical appearance, and she should pay attention to her husband's physical appearance too. As I said before, a wife should take an interest in every area of her husband's life and support him in every way possible to help him do what God has called him to do. Your husband will feel better about himself when he knows he looks his best. And feeling good about himself will help him do his job better.

I have seen the way some ministers have looked, and I've wondered if their wives paid any attention to their husbands' clothes at all. As a usual thing, men aren't as good as women at putting a wardrobe together and knowing when something is too old or frayed to wear.

Their minds are usually on other things more than on clothes.

I go shopping with Kenneth because he's not the best at matching colors and coordinating a wardrobe. I enjoy doing that for him and helping him decide which clothes to buy. Helping Kenneth like this is one way I support him when he goes out to minister to others.

There are many practical ways you can support your husband and help him be the best he can be. Supporting your husband's call is more than just praying for your husband, although prayer is probably the most important thing you can do for him. But sometimes it's doing the little things that really minister to your husband and show him you love and care about him.

For instance, how many of you wives give your husband a kiss before he leaves for work in the morning and when he returns from work in the evening? If you don't do this, you should. Some wives work with their husbands, and they are with their husbands all day long. But if that is the case, how many times have you just walked up to your husband during the day and kissed him and said, "I sure do love you. You're valuable and precious to me, and I support you in everything you're doing for the Lord"?

A husband needs to know his wife loves and admires him. He needs to know his wife respects him and looks up to him. And as a wife, you need to tell your husband often that you love him and care about him and that you're interested in every area of his life. In *The Amplified Bible*, First Peter 3:2 says a wife is to reverence her husband — "to respect, defer to, revere him; [revere means] to honor, esteem (appreciate, prize), and [in the human sense] adore him; [and adore means] to admire, praise, be devoted to, deeply love and enjoy [your husband]."

Don't we wish we could all measure up to that? I wish I could say I've always been that way, but I can't. None of us can. But we *can* all grow and develop in God's Word and continually become more and more what God wants us to be. God wants us to live godly lives before our husbands (1 Peter 3:1).

I have discussed this subject of supporting your husband's call with many women's groups, and I have often heard the comment, "Well, I'm a minister too. Why should I do those things for my husband. I'm just as important as he is. He should be doing those things for *me*."

It's not a matter of who is more important. Your husband is the head of your home, and you need to treat him like he is the head. Some women think their careers and their desires should come first, and they want to put *themselves* first in their marriage instead of putting their mate first.

But that attitude is very wrong. And if you feel that way, you need to pray a little more and let God talk to your heart a little more. Certainly, a wife has needs, and her husband should minister to her needs too. Both the husband and wife have responsibilities and neither one of them should neglect their responsibilities. But, wives, if you will see to it that you obey God and do your part, God will reward you. Obedience and faithfulness to God and His Word always pays.

I always wanted to put my husband first in our marriage. I felt it was my duty to encourage him in his calling in life and to "hold his hands up" and support him. A husband needs to be lifted up and encouraged, and he needs to know that you, his wife, are standing with him and that you believe in him. He needs to know that even when times are hard, he's got one person in the world who is standing with him and who will believe in him regardless of the circumstances that may come his way.

As I said before, a wife can either *make* or *break* her husband. So why not be an asset to your husband's life and help him be the best he can be? Tell your husband often that you love him and that you're thankful God gave him to you. Tell him that he's the only one in the world for you and that you wouldn't have it any other way. Speaking words of love and encouragement will go a long way in showing your support for your husband and in bringing harmony and fulfillment into your marriage too. And God will richly reward your obedience as you faithfully support your husband's call.

Chapter 5
My Personal Journey
Of Faith

It is difficult sometimes to sense when spiritual changes take place in your own life. Spiritual growth is something that just develops from the inside, from your heart, through your knowledge and understanding of God and His Word.

It seems many times I've noticed spiritual changes in my life when I faced a difficult situation and had to use my own faith to overcome the test or trial. There were many times I couldn't see how we were going to make it in the natural through some of the hard times we faced in the ministry.

But God is faithful even in the hard places. And it's in the hard places in life that the Holy Spirit will guide you in greater and greater ways if you will look to Him to help you. Always look to the Word and to your recreated spirit for answers to problems in life. The Holy Spirit will guide you through your spirit, and He will always guide you in line with the Word of God.

I have always depended on the Lord to guide me, especially in the hard places in life. There were many situations over the years that if it were up to me, I would have gone another way, in another direction, instead of going the way the Lord wanted us to go. But I always knew the Lord was leading and guiding us, and I trusted Him.

I trusted my husband too. But there were times I had to make decisions on my own, without Kenneth, because he was on the road ministering. During those times, I would just look to the Lord, and He always helped me. Sometimes the Lord would say to me, "Do it this way. Remember, I will never leave you or forsake you," and He would show me what to do.

The Lord is so sweet, and I'm so glad I obeyed Him. I'm so glad that in the hard places, I did things His way and not my own way, because He has never failed me. The Lord has seen me through some problems that seemed impossible to solve in the natural. But He gave me the grace and the wisdom to handle each problem, and He always saw me through the difficult times.

Being alone while Kenneth was ministering on the road gave me some wonderful opportunities to use my faith to grow in my walk with the Lord. It's so important to develop your own faith life because the hard times come to us all. But when we are walking with Jesus every day, doing what He wants us to do, the faith life works, because God is faithful.

Developing your faith life means you have to study God's Word and pray. It means you have to take time seeking the Lord. And it doesn't happen overnight. When people see Kenneth's ministry today, they might think he has always had it easy. But we didn't start at the top in the ministry — we started at the bottom! Kenneth spent many long hours early in his ministry studying the Word and praying and seeking God. And he has continued to do that over the years. Kenneth has been faithful to preach the message of faith in God's Word, even in the hard times when every circumstance seemed to be against us.

My husband is a quiet man, and he has always been a man of prayer. Everyone who knows Kenneth knows he just doesn't talk a lot. But when he wants to talk, you listen, because you know you'll learn something if you do. I always tell people not to let their feelings get hurt if he doesn't say much to them. Kenneth just doesn't talk a lot.

Someone said, "Well, I couldn't live like that if I were you." Yes, you could. And you could learn something from a person like Kenneth who doesn't talk a lot. I've always said, you can learn a lot more by listening and keeping quiet than by talking all the time!

The Bible says, ". . . you married women, be submissive to your own husbands . . . and adapt yourselves to them . . ." (1 Peter 3:1 *Amp.*). I adapted myself to my husband, and over the years I have learned a lot about the things of God from him. Kenneth has always been very diligent to read and study the Word and pray. Since we were first married, Kenneth has always set aside times of study and prayer, and I never minded. I was glad my husband walked closely with the Lord.

I've often been asked, "Did you ever feel neglected when your husband spent time studying and praying?" No, I never did feel neglected. And I never nagged Kenneth or interrupted him in his studies. I always supported my husband in whatever he did for the Lord.

And Kenneth has always been very thoughtful of me and attentive to my needs.

I had my own times of studying and praying because many times while Kenneth was spending time alone with God, I would use that time to be alone with God too. Fellowship with God is so important in building a strong faith life. The further along Kenneth and I went in the ministry, the more I realized that those times I spent alone with God paid great dividends.

Prayer was an important part of supporting my husband's ministry. I used every opportunity I could to pray for Kenneth and his ministry. I didn't always have a special time set aside just to pray. Many times I would pray while I worked around the house, just talking to God and lifting the situations of Kenneth's life up before the Lord.

As I said, prayer and fellowship with God is important in developing your faith life. But you can't develop your faith with just prayer. You need the Word, too, because faith comes by hearing the Word (Rom. 10:17). Then once faith comes, you must *use* your faith in order for it to work for you. You've got to *work* your faith, and that's how faith gets stronger and stronger.

When you start out working your faith, you don't have to start out big — just use your faith where you are at in your spiritual walk. Spiritual growth is a lot like physical growth, and no one starts out in life full grown. You may not start out using your faith for big things. But if you are faithful to God and His Word, the little things you start out using your faith for will grow and become greater. And that pleases God because when you are using faith, it shows you are trusting Him.

Kenneth and I didn't start out at the top in our faith walk. In fact, we started out in the ministry with nothing. We lived by faith every day. Kenneth and I bought our first house by faith. It was a small three-bedroom frame house in Garland, Texas, and it was a very nice house for that day. We had been renting the house, but then we bought it.

Kenneth and I used our faith to get that house. I remember I wanted new drapes for our new home, but when I said something to Kenneth about it, he said, "Honey, I've already extended my faith as far as it will go right now. I can't believe for any more than I'm believing for right now. You'll just have to believe God for the drapes yourself." I did, and God provided us with the drapes I wanted!

Over the years I've had many opportunities to learn how to use my own faith. Kenneth couldn't carry me with his faith forever because God requires every one of us to grow in faith and stand on His Word for ourselves. God wants us to grow up and not remain spiritual babies.

So there came a time in my life when Kenneth could no longer carry me with his faith. And I'm so glad he couldn't because it made me develop a faith life of my own. I didn't know how important that would be until 1963 when the devil tried to attack me in my body with sickness. I lost ten pounds in one week, and I became weak and nervous. I went to my family doctor, and he ran some tests. The doctor was alarmed by the results, and he wanted me to see a specialist.

I didn't want to go to the specialist because I didn't really want to find out what was wrong with me; I didn't want to hear any bad news. When a doctor tells you that you have to see a specialist, if you're like I was at that time, you're just not too anxious to go and find out what's wrong! (I learned better since then, because that's not always a wise thing to do. But at that time, I just didn't want to know what the specialist might find wrong with me.)

So after I had the tests, I went home. I didn't tell my doctor whether I would go to the specialist or not. The children were grown at that time. Pat was married and Ken Jr. had gone into the military service. Kenneth was away holding meetings, and I was home alone.

One afternoon shortly after I had gone to the doctor, the Lord spoke to my husband while he was in another town holding a meeting. Kenneth was lying across the bed, studying in the room where he was staying, and the Lord said, "Go call your wife and tell her to go to the specialist."

Kenneth said, "Okay, Lord, I'll do that tonight." And the Lord said, "Go call her *now*." So Kenneth got up and phoned me, and I immediately called my doctor to make an appointment for me to see the specialist.

I immediately went to the specialist, and he put me through test after test. The last test he gave me was a five-hour glucose tolerance test. Every hour I had to drink glucose, a type of sugary syrup. It was supposed to make my blood sugar rise, but it didn't. Instead, mine went down. And every hour it continued to go down.

During the test, I would become so weak the nurses would have to help me get to a bed so I could lie down awhile before they could finish the test. The specialist later told Kenneth that my condition was so serious, he thought I would die at any minute.

The doctor told Kenneth, "I monitored her reaction each time she drank the glucose. The last time she drank it, I said to myself, *If her blood sugar doesn't come up this time, she could die.*" But the last time I drank the glucose, my blood sugar came up a little.

After all the testing, the doctor told me I had hypo-glycemia, which is also known as low blood sugar. He said to me, "You have the worse case I have ever seen." Later he told my husband, "It was wise to have her come to me when she did because she got here just in time."

God was so merciful and kind to speak to my husband the way He did and tell Kenneth that I should see the specialist. God met me where I was at in my spiritual walk, but He still expected me to grow in faith.

Before all this happened, we were holding a meeting in a church in south Texas. I had gone to our room to rest one afternoon before the evening meeting. Kenneth went over to the church to pray. When he came back to the room, he woke me and said, "It's late. You'd better get up and get ready."

"Okay," I answered him, still half asleep. But when he left the room, I didn't get up. I went back to sleep.

Kenneth woke me up again, but I still didn't get up.
The third time Kenneth tried to wake me, he had to get
me out of bed and walk me around the room in order to
wake me up.

The doctor told us that happened because I was laps-
ing into a coma due to low blood sugar. He said if Kenneth hadn't wakened me, I could have gone into a coma
and never come out of it.

The specialist sent me home and told me not to do
anything unless it was absolutely necessary. I was so
weak, the doctor didn't want me to use up any extra
energy at all. I had to stay in bed, and I had to eat certain foods six times a day, at the very hours the doctor
told me to eat them.

I followed the doctor's instructions, and I also began
taking medication. I would get better, but then I would
get worse again. You might ask, "Well, Brother Hagin is
a man of faith, and he teaches healing. Couldn't he pray
the prayer of faith for you?" No, he couldn't. Baby
Christians can often get healed by someone else's faith,
but sooner or later, God wants them to stand on their
own, and they will have to use their own faith. You can't
always ride on somebody else's faith.

At that particular time, I was so weak, it was hard
for me to use my own faith. Have you ever been to the
place where you were too weak to grasp the truth of
God's Word and use your faith? I was at that place, so
at first, I would just lie in bed and read the Bible.

When I became stronger, I began to stand on Mark
11:24: *"Therefore I say unto you, What things soever ye*

desire, when ye pray, believe that ye receive them, and ye shall have them." I prayed for my healing, but that wasn't all I did. Mark 11:24 says, "*. . . when ye pray, BELIEVE THAT YE RECEIVE THEM, and ye shall have them.*" So I prayed, but I also *believed I received* my healing. You see, you can pray and pray and pray about something, but if you don't believe you receive, you won't ever have it.

Even after I prayed, I continued to struggle with low blood sugar. I'd get better one day, and then I'd be weak the next day — so weak I'd have to stay home and rest. Sometimes I didn't even have enough energy to go to church.

I had always gone to church services with my husband before, and I had always prayed for him and supported him as he ministered in his meetings. The two of us are one. I am a part of Kenneth, and even though I am not a preacher, his ministry is my ministry, too, because we are one. And I've always supported my husband in the ministry.

But even though I was very weak at times, I continued to use my faith for healing. As I said, Kenneth could not have received my healing for me because I had been sitting under the teaching of the Word in healing meetings for years. I should have been to the place where I could receive my healing for myself, but my faith wasn't developed to that place right then.

All healings are not instant. Actually, most healings are gradual. That's why you have to keep your confession right. You can't have a confession today, "By Jesus' stripes I'm healed," but then the next day say, "I don't know if I'm healed or not." You will never get your healing that way. You have to hold on to your confession in God's Word in order for faith to work for you.

The sickness in my body went on for about a year. I'd get better, but then I would get worse. But I continued to believe God, and my faith grew stronger and stronger every day.

Then one night, Kenneth and I were in a meeting in Fort Worth, Texas, and the Lord spoke to me. That day I'd had a battle with my thoughts all day long. I was weak and nervous, and the devil kept saying to me, "You're going to die! You're going to die!"

Finally, I got so mad at the devil, I said, "Devil, I'm not going to die. I'm going to live! The Word of God says, '. . . *What things soever ye desire, when ye pray, believe that ye receive them, and ye shall have them.*' I believe I'm healed and I'm not going to die." Sometimes you have to get to the place where you get mad at the devil and stand your ground on the Word.

That evening during the service as we were praising and worshipping the Lord, the Lord said to me so sweetly, "You are healed." It was so sweet and precious, and I just began to rejoice to think my faith had grown to the place where I could receive my healing.

It's wonderful when the Lord speaks to you, but that doesn't mean you're supposed to sit around and listen for the Lord to talk to you like that, because He may never do it. It's our business to stand on the Word, and it's God's business to do the work. He may speak to us, and He may not. But we always have His Word.

I don't know why the Lord spoke to me that way. I didn't question it, I just praised Him for it. I went home that night and slept good. I didn't take any more medicine for hypoglycemia, and from that day to this, I have never had any more problems with low blood sugar!

But my healing hadn't been an instant thing. It had taken me from June until September of the next year — over a year — before my faith was developed to receive my healing. But that doesn't mean healing has to take that long.

The Bible says that by Jesus' stripes we are *already* healed (1 Peter 2:24). But sometimes God has to get you to a place of faith where you can receive what you need from Him. That's not the best way. The best way is to already be at that place of faith when a crisis comes. That's why it's so important to put the Word inside you and *keep* it inside you. Then when the tests and trials come, you will have something to draw from, and you can stand in faith and receive whatever it is you need from God.

Some people think God puts sickness on people to teach them something. But God doesn't put sickness on people. That's the devil's business. The devil will try to ruin a person's life and ministry if he can — any way he can, including with sickness and disease. The devil will try to come into a person's life through every door he can in order to try to block what God wants for that person's life. But we don't have to put up with the devil and his works.

If you are sick, God wants to heal you. God does not want you to be sick. If you are suffering with sickness in your body right now, don't keep wondering, "Why me? Why has this come upon me?" If that is your attitude, I know exactly how you feel because I went through that too. But you've got to get beyond that point if you want to receive from God. You can't receive from God if you're having a pity party and feeling sorry for yourself all the time. You've got to concentrate on getting the Word into your spirit, not just in your head, in order for it to work for you. And you can't do that if you permit self-pity to be in your life.

Whatever you're seeking from God, the Word has got to be in your spirit in order for you to receive what you want. So don't let anything stand in your way of putting God's Word in your heart or spirit. If you don't keep God's Word alive in your spirit, your faith will be hindered and you won't be able to receive what you need from God.

Sometimes our faith can also be hindered by fear. But fear is from the devil, not from God. And if you let fear take ahold of you, you are giving place to the devil, not to God. If you will trust God and give place to *God* when you're in a spiritual battle, God will deliver you. God is so gracious and faithful to every one of His children, no matter who you are.

Sometimes it's in the middle of a test or trial when we really come to know God's grace and His faithfulness. The Lord is so good, and He loves us so much. Sometimes we don't realize how good God is until a crisis comes and He helps us through it. God will always answer us when we stay true to His Word and trust Him. But we have to show ourselves faithful to Him and His Word both in the good times and in the hard times.

Whether we want to believe it or not, the hard times will come. Tests and trials come to everyone at some time or another. None of us get to float through life on flowery beds of ease. But if you are faithful to God and His Word, then when the tests and trials come, you will have something to draw from because you will have God's Word in your heart. And God's Word never fails.

In 1984, I went through another severe test of my faith due to sickness. But God was so faithful, and He saw me through it.

I had a blockage in my heart that caused me a lot of pain, and it left me weak and exhausted all the time. When my doctor ran tests and told me what was wrong, I was frightened at first. But I didn't just sit down and wait for Kenneth to pray for me and not use my own faith. Yes, Kenneth prayed for me, but he couldn't get my healing for me. I had to do it myself — just me and God.

I had been very tired for about eight months before I went to the doctor for tests and found out what was wrong with me. I thought I was just tired because we had been so busy. We'd had a very busy schedule that summer with crusades. But finally I became so weak, I couldn't even walk across the room without help.

When I finally went to the doctor for a checkup, he

said I had a heart blockage and that the blood wasn't flowing through one side of my heart. He was very concerned. He ordered more tests to see if an operation was necessary or if I could take medicine for the condition. He told me to go home and go to bed and not to do anything strenuous because he said my heart couldn't take it.

When the doctor first told me the news, I guess he saw that I looked frightened because he quoted me the scripture, *"For God hath not given us the spirit of fear; but of power, and of love, and of a sound mind"* (2 Tim. 1:7). It was so good to have a Christian doctor. After he quoted that scripture, he prayed a beautiful prayer for me. Others prayed for me, too, although we didn't tell too many people about it.

When Kenneth came home from the office on the day I received the diagnosis, he asked me, "Well, what did the doctor say? What report did he give you?" When I told him I had a blockage in my heart, he turned white as a sheet, and I thought he was going to faint. That was his first reaction, but then we immediately looked to the Lord.

I knew my husband was strong in faith and that he would stand with me for my healing. And Kenneth did pray for me and believe God with me. But I also knew I had to be strong in faith too. I had to know for myself who my Healer is. The most important thing to know when sickness tries to attack you is that *Jesus* is your Healer. You've got to know Jesus for *yourself*.

I'm so glad I knew Jesus when that crisis came. My

husband has had a tremendous healing ministry for many years, but I still knew he could not get my healing for me. I had to get into the Word and stand on the Word myself. So I began to feed God's Word into my spirit. Kenneth had recorded a cassette tape called "Healing Scriptures" which I listened to constantly, and I meditated on the Word day in and day out. I built myself up in faith.

Healing doesn't come to you just because you have faith. You've got to *work* your faith. It's got to be in your heart, not just in your head, and you have to use your faith in line with the Word. Just believing is not enough. You've got to tell God what you believe, and you've got to tell the devil what you believe. You've got to *say* what you believe.

We had a crusade scheduled in California at that time. I promised my doctor I would get enough rest, so he finally agreed to let me go to the crusade with my husband. Kenneth wouldn't let me go to the services in the daytime. I stayed in our room and rested. I'd have lunch with Kenneth, and I'd rest in the afternoon. Then I'd go to the evening services and help Kenneth minister.

As long as I was under the anointing of the Holy Spirit in the services, I felt fine. But when the anointing began to wear off, the pain would start again. Sometimes the pain was so severe, I thought I wouldn't be able to stand it for another minute. And I was so weak, I could hardly walk across the room.

But I kept using my faith. I did not give up. Yes, I rested because I had enough sense to know that if I didn't rest, my heart couldn't take it. So I rested, but I never quit using my faith.

Certainly, using my faith was a battle. It was not easy. The devil tried to fight me every step of the way. It seemed the devil would hop on my shoulder and say, "What are you going to do now? You're the wife of a prophet and healing minister. You're not going to get healed. What's that going to do to your husband's ministry?"

I would always answer, "It's not going to do anything to my husband's ministry because I'm *not* going to die. Besides, whether I get my healing or not, God's Word is still true."

When the devil would talk to me and try to scare me with his lies, I didn't just sit down and start crying; I resisted him. I kept listening to Kenneth's healing tape. I also read the Word and prayed. I'd get up in the morning listening to that healing scriptures tape, and I'd go to bed listening to it. Every minute I possibly could, I had that tape on, and I listened to it and kept God's Word alive in my spirit.

Don't ever think that just because you're standing on the Word that the devil will leave you alone, because he won't. He will be there every minute with his doubt and unbelief, trying to make you quit and give up on your faith. But don't quit! God is faithful, and He will never fail you if you are trusting Him and being faithful to His Word.

I had been battling with that heart condition since April. We returned from our crusade in December, and I was scheduled to go back to the doctor for more tests. One evening as Kenneth and I were sitting in our living room at home, I just began to meditate on the Scriptures. I knew that in order to get my healing, the Word had to be in my spirit or heart, not just in my head.

As I sat there in my living room meditating on the Scriptures and thinking about the goodness of God, suddenly I felt what seemed like two hands reaching down into my heart. It was the Holy Spirit. Those hands lifted something out of my heart and set it down beside the chair. Right then I knew my healing was complete — that the full manifestation had come. Tears began to roll down my cheeks as I quietly thanked God for His goodness and His love. I was so happy!

It was so sweet and so sacred to think God loved me enough to do that for me. But He *does* love me that much, and He loves you the same way. God doesn't love one of His children more than He does another. He is so wonderful and gracious to every one of us who will put our trust in Him.

Sitting there in my living room that evening, I was so touched by God's love for me that at first I couldn't even tell my husband what happened to me. I could only share my joy with the Lord, for it was He who had healed me. Kenneth had been sitting in the living room with me, watching the evening news on television. Later, as we walked down the hall arm-in-arm to the bedroom, I said, "Honey, I've got something to tell you." I told him my healing was complete, and we rejoiced together at what the Lord had done.

I went back to the doctor for more tests, and when the nurse called me about a week later with the results, she told me, "Mrs. Hagin, all of your tests have come back negative." Then the doctor wanted Kenneth and me to come to his office to meet with him. We did, and when we came into his office, the doctor just looked at me and said, "I want you to know there is nothing wrong with your heart. Your heart is perfect in every way. You don't need medication, and you don't need any surgery. Your heart is perfect, and you can tell people your doctor said so."

Our doctor was a Christian, and he had seen many patients recover with the help of both prayer and medicine. But he told us that my healing was the first bona fide miracle he'd ever personally seen.

Someone asked, "Weren't you nervous when you had to go back to the doctor for more tests? Weren't you afraid the doctor was going to find something still wrong with your heart?" No, I wasn't nervous or afraid at all because I knew God had done the work and that my healing was complete. I knew God's Word is true and that He had touched me, and nobody could tell me any different.

I knew in my heart that I was healed, and nobody could take that knowledge away from me. But my heart didn't get healed because I'm in the ministry or because I'm the wife of a prophet and healing minister. I could not have received my healing if I had just been sitting around all those years, not putting God's Word in my spirit. Yes, God is always ready to heal us. But we have a part to play too. As I said, if we are faithful to God's Word, He will be faithful to us. But if we don't honor God's Word and stand on His Word, He doesn't have anything to make good in our lives.

Many people don't take the time with God's Word that they should. They don't hide God's Word in their hearts (Ps. 119:11), and when a crisis comes, they don't have anything to draw from. Yes, some people receive instant healings and miracles because God is merciful. But most of the time, healings are not instant. So it's wise to know how to stand your ground on God's Word and use your own faith.

God never puts sickness on people, and He never says, "Wait," when you ask Him to heal you. God is *always* ready to heal and bless His people. But many times, God has to get us to the place where we are in faith before He can move in our lives like He wants to. He has to prepare us to receive from Him because we receive from God by *faith*, and there's really no other way.

That's why it's so important to give God's Word first place in your life. Don't wait for the crisis or the test or trial before you start putting God's Word in your heart because then it might be too late. But if you are faithful to God and His Word, He will always see you through any test or trial.

Being faithful to God and living by faith is not always easy. Many times in my life, I thought it would be so much easier to do things my own way or just give up and not obey what the Lord had told us to do.

Many of you may be feeling that way now. You may be facing tests and trials that you think you can't overcome. You may be thinking, *It's just too hard to fight anymore. I just can't go on.* But don't give up. There's nothing too hard for God. It's too hard for you in your own strength. But with God, nothing is impossible. So put your eyes on Jesus! He's the One who's going to see you through anyway. You can't do it yourself. But if you will be faithful to Him and do what He's told you to do, the answer will always come.

Yes, you have a part to play in receiving the blessings of God. You have to be faithful to God and His Word. But nothing is more rewarding in life than to stay faithful to God and to be faithful to put His Word in your heart. Then you can do what God wants you to do and be a blessing to others. You will never be sorry for remaining faithful to God and to His will and His plan for your life because pay day always comes to those who are faithful.

My husband has often said that if you will stay put in the hard places in life, you will eventually rest on the mountaintop. By God's grace Kenneth and I have stayed put in the hard places. We have stayed faithful to the plan of God for our lives. There was a price to pay to stay put when the times were hard. But we paid the price willingly. We always counted it a privilege to serve God in the ministry and to fulfill His plan for our lives.

And the plan continues to unfold! We are excited about what the future holds for us because we serve a faithful God. And we are thankful for God's grace and His faithfulness in the past because of what He has

already enabled us to accomplish in the ministry. At each phase of our ministry, we didn't always understand as we do now everything God had planned for us. But we followed the Lord step-by-step, counting Him faithful. And we found that His grace was greater than any price we had to pay.